Everyday Abiding: 40 Days of Living Fully in Christ

Kurt Barnes

Copyright © 2024 Kurt Barnes

All rights reserved.

ISBN: 9798303174412

DEDICATION

To my beloved wife, Summer, whose unwavering support and love make every journey worthwhile.

To my children, Keegan and Kyler, whose laughter and curiosity teach me daily about the depth of the Father's love for us.

To my parents, Rob and Kathy, for their lifelong love, guidance, and wisdom.

And to my Silver Creek Fellowship Church family. Thank you for your constant prayers, love, and for walking this journey with me.

CONTENTS

A JOURNEY INTO ABIDING   7

JOHN 15-THE HEART OF ABIDING   9

WEEK 1: FOUNDATIONS OF ABIDING

Day 1: Abiding as Connection   11

Day 2: Abiding in Love   14

Day 3: The Necessity of Abiding   16

Day 4: Abiding over Anxiety   19

Day 5: Christ as the Vine   22

Day 6: Detached Without Christ   25

Day 7: Abiding through Discipleship   28

Week 1: Small Group Guide   31

WEEK 2: ABIDING IN PRACTICE

Day 8: Abiding in the Word   34

Day 9: Abiding in Prayer   38

Day 10: Abiding in Community   41

Day 11: Abiding in Worship   44

Day 12: Abiding with the Spirit   47

Day 13: Abiding amid Busyness   50

Day 14: Abiding through Obedience   53

Week 2: Small Group Guide   56

WEEK 3: DEEPENING THE ABIDING

Day 15: Abiding through Reflection   59

Day 16: Abiding through Trials   62

Day 17: Abiding and Simplicity   65

Day 18: Abiding through Service   68

Day 19: Abiding in God's Promises   71

Day 20: Abiding with Humility   74

Day 21: Abiding through Rest   77

Week 3: Small Group Guide   80

WEEK 4: TRANSFORMATIVE ABIDING

Day 22: Abiding and Transformation   83

Day 23: Abiding in Mission   86

Day 24: Abiding in Fruitfulness   89

Day 25: Abiding amid Doubt   92

Day 26: Abiding in God's Timing   95

Day 27: Abiding and Renewal   98

Day 28: Abiding as a Lifestyle   102

Week 4: Small Group Guide   105

WEEK 5: LIVING ABIDING EVERY DAY

Day 29: Abiding with Gratitude   108

Day 30: Abiding and Generosity   111

Day 31: Abiding and Honesty   114

Day 32: Abiding through Listening   117

Day 33: Abiding in God's Strength   120

Day 34: Abiding and Trust   123

Day 35: Abiding and Reconciliation   126

Week 5: Small Group Guide   129

WEEK 6: CONTINUAL ABIDING

Day 36: Abiding through Forgiveness   132

Day 37: Abiding in Rest Revisited   135

Day 38: Abiding and Vision   138

Day 39: Continuously Abiding   141

Day 40: Abiding in Christ's Future   144

Week 6: Small Group Guide   147

CONCLUSION   149

A JOURNEY INTO ABIDING

"'The time of busyness does not with me differ from the time of prayer; and in the noise and clatter of my kitchen, while several persons are at the same time calling for different things, I possess God in as great tranquility as if I were upon my knees at the Blessed Sacrament.'" — Brother Lawrence

Imagine standing alongside Brother Lawrence in his hectic kitchen, surrounded by pots clanging and voices calling out amid the sizzle and steam. Yet, amidst this chaos, he finds an abiding serenity, a profound presence of God that sustains him through every clattering moment. His approach reveals a faith immersed in life's noise, teaching us that abiding in Christ transforms even the busiest moments into sacred encounters.

In today's world, faith often becomes a task among many—a checkbox on our to-do lists, neatly tucked away between the routines of work, family, and social obligations. We reserve our spiritual lives for Sundays or limited times of reflection, cordoning off sacred from secular. However, this separation dilutes the vibrant potential of our faith to infuse and transform our everyday lives.

What if the key to a fulfilled, vibrant faith is not compartmentalization, but integration—allowing our spiritual lives to seamlessly blend with our daily experiences? Abiding in Christ calls us to this revelation, inviting a dynamic journey where each moment becomes an opportunity to dwell deeply in God's presence. It challenges us to embrace every aspect of life as both holy and complete, allowing faith to infiltrate every thought, action, and interaction.

Picture the shift when faith becomes a continuous thread woven through everything we do. Relationships deepen, challenges become transformative, and daily moments turn into expressions of God's love and grace. Abiding isn't about achieving perfection; it's about letting Christ be the core of your existence, nurturing strength and wisdom throughout your journey.

Abiding in Christ is more than a concept—it's a life-oriented approach where His presence guides, strengthens, and transforms us. This journey is not solely about learning or doing; it transcends these to become an intimate experience: to stay, dwell, and be at peace in Christ. Through abiding, our lives become living testaments to God's love, grace, and truth, reaching out to the world around us.

JOHN 15-THE HEART OF ABIDING

John 15:1-8 (ESV)

"I am the true vine, and my Father is the vinedresser. 2 Every branch in me that does not bear fruit he takes away, and every branch that does bear fruit he prunes, that it may bear more fruit. 3 Already you are clean because of the word that I have spoken to you. 4 Abide in me, and I in you. As the branch cannot bear fruit by itself, unless it abides in the vine, neither can you, unless you abide in me. 5 I am the vine; you are the branches. Whoever abides in me and I in him, he it is that bears much fruit, for apart from me you can do nothing. 6 If anyone does not abide in me he is thrown away like a branch and withers; and the branches are gathered, thrown into the fire, and burned. 7 If you abide in me, and my words abide in you, ask whatever you wish, and it will be done for you. 8 By this my Father is glorified, that you bear much fruit and so prove to be my disciples.

In the tapestry of scripture, John 15 stands out as a profound invitation and promise. Jesus' words are not only a reminder of our connection with Him but also a blueprint for a life fully rooted in God's presence. As believers, we often find solace in these verses, hearing the call to "abide in me, and I in you" (John 15:4). While we recognize its importance, many of us struggle with translating this ideal into our daily lives.

The metaphor of the vine and branches vividly illustrates this call. Jesus identifies Himself as the true vine, the source of all spiritual nourishment. We, the branches, draw life and strength from our connection to Him. This connection is fundamental; apart from Him, we can do nothing. Abiding is not a passive state. It is an active, conscious choice to remain in Him, to dwell continuously in His love and guidance, allowing His life to flow through us.

John 15 speaks to the heart of spiritual vitality and growth. In these passages, Jesus assures us that abiding in Him produces fruit—acts of love, expressions of joy, and moments of grace that reflect His character in and through us. This fruitfulness is evidence of a true abiding relationship, one where the divine intertwines seamlessly with our human journey.

Yet, as straightforward as this call may seem, understanding "how" to abide remains complex in the rhythm of daily living. Our lives fast-track through responsibilities, demands, and distractions that threaten to pull us away from this vital connection. We often wonder how to maintain an abiding spirit amidst noisy schedules and relentless priorities. The challenge lies in integrating this sacred relationship with Christ into every moment, transforming the ordinary into extraordinary expressions of faith.

The struggle is universal, yet the yearning for a deeper connection with Christ persists. Many of us know we should abide, we feel its necessity, but the "how" often remains elusive. Our challenge, therefore, is to bridge this gap, finding practical ways to dwell continuously in His presence.

Over the next 40 days, this exploration invites you into a rhythm where spiritual practices, reflection, and real-world engagement intersect, breathing life into the essence of abiding. Together, we will delve into principles and practices designed to nurture deep intimacy with Christ and transcend traditional spiritual practices into a lifestyle of continuous communion.

Expect each day's journey to begin with a principle that opens new dimensions of abiding, followed by a practice that offers tangible steps to integrate these truths into your daily walk. From quiet reflections to active engagements, these practices aim to anchor these teachings in your life and reveal the transformative power of abiding in Christ.

Let this be an invitation to step into a life alive with possibility. Envision transformation that extends beyond yourself, touching lives and shaping communities in ways previously unimaginable. Let His rhythm of love, grace, and truth encompass every moment. Here begins a journey—not just of understanding but of becoming—rooting deeper into the life God envisions for you. Together, let's embrace a transformative path of abiding.

WEEK 1: FOUNDATIONS OF ABIDING

Day 1: Abiding as Connection

Principle: Abiding as Connection

In our walk with Christ, the analogy of a vine and branches is paramount. Jesus instructs, "I am the vine; you are the branches. If you remain in me and I in you, you will bear much fruit; apart from me, you can do nothing" (John 15:5, NIV). This powerful image captures the essence of dependency and nourishment found solely in Christ. Just as branches draw sustenance from the vine, our lives flourish when deeply rooted in Him.

The Apostle Paul echoes this truth, urging the Colossians to "continue to live your lives in him, rooted and built up in him" (Colossians 2:6-7, NIV). This imagery of rootedness implies stability and growth, a continuous cultivation of our inner life sustained by Christ.

In a culture that often values independence, the call to abide is countercultural. It challenges the notion of self-reliance, inviting us instead into a rhythm of reliance on God. Abiding is not passive; it actively shapes our thoughts, actions, and priorities, aligning them with divine purpose.

Consider the life of Jesus, who modeled a life of abiding through prayer and intentional withdrawals to spend time with the Father (Matthew 14:23, Mark 1:35). His earthly ministry was empowered by His profound connection with God, demonstrating that solitude with God fuels public ministry and daily interactions.

The challenge of abiding is heightened by modern distractions. Yet, just as the early church persevered through adversity by anchoring firmly in Christ's teachings and community, we too can find resilience in the stability of abiding. The vitality of this connection manifests in peace and purpose amidst the noise of life.

As we embark on this journey, prioritize creating space for abiding in everyday routines. Devote time to reading Scripture, prayer, and meditation, reflecting on God's promises. Practically invite Jesus into every decision and interaction, seeking His wisdom and guidance. Cultivate a habit of gratitude, giving thanks for moments of awareness of His presence.

Reflect on Brother Lawrence's wisdom, adopting a posture of perceiving God's presence in every task, whether mundane or monumental. Let your everyday actions become expressions of prayer and worship, embodying the truth that each moment is sacred when anchored in Christ.

Abiding transforms the ordinary into sacred encounters, enriching our lives and interactions. Today, commit to nurturing this connection, trusting in God's sustaining grace to navigate your journey with strength and serenity. As you remain in Him, anticipate bearing the fruit of His Spirit, radiating love, joy, peace, and hope to those around you.

Abiding Practice: Quiet Reflection on Scripture

In today's practice, you'll embrace the foundational principle of "Abiding as Connection" by immersing yourself in the life-giving words of Scripture. This quiet reflection will help you deepen your understanding of what it means to remain connected to Christ and draw strength from His presence.

Practice: Quiet Reflection on John 15:4-5

1. **Find a Quiet Place**: Select a peaceful location where you can focus without distractions. This might be your favorite chair, a quiet park bench, or any space that feels calming and allows for quietude.

2. **Prepare Your Heart**: Begin by taking a few deep breaths to center yourself. As you breathe in, invite the Holy Spirit to guide your thoughts and open your heart to receive God's message. Breathe out any distractions or concerns, making space for divine focus.

3. **Read the Scripture**: Slowly read John 15:4-5 aloud, letting each word resonate:
"Remain in me, as I also remain in you. No branch can bear fruit by itself; it must remain in the vine. Neither can you bear fruit unless you remain in me. I am the vine; you are the branches."

4. **Reflect and Meditate**: Spend a few moments reflecting on the imagery Jesus presents. Visualize yourself as a branch firmly

connected to the vine. Consider what it means for your life to draw nourishment, strength, and purpose from Christ.

5. **Ask Reflective Questions**: Inwardly ask yourself:
    - How does my life reflect the connection with Christ?
    - Are there areas where I feel disconnected or self-reliant?
    - What fruit am I bearing as a result of my relationship with Him?

6. **Listen and Absorb**: Sit quietly, allowing God's words to permeate your heart. Be attentive to any thoughts, feelings, or impressions that arise as you meditate on this truth. Allow yourself to rest in the assurance of His continuous presence.

7. **Conclude with Prayer**: End your time with a short prayer of response:
"Lord Jesus, thank You for being my source of strength and life. Help me to stay connected to You today and always, drawing from Your wisdom and love. Teach me to abide and bear fruit that glorifies Your name. Amen."

8. **Carry It Forward**: Embrace the insights gained during this reflection, carrying them into your day. Let the awareness of your connection to Christ guide your actions, decisions, and interactions.

This practice is an invitation to linger in God's presence, allowing His Word to live within you and inspire a life deeply rooted in Him. As you continually return to this reflection, you will find a greater sense of peace and purpose flowing from your abiding connection with Christ.

WEEK 1: FOUNDATIONS OF ABIDING

Day 2: Abiding in Love

Principle: Abiding in Love

To abide in Christ is to dwell in His love—the core of our faith journey. This love is not just a comforting assurance but an active, transformative force shaping our identity and guiding our actions. Jesus clearly imparts this truth: "As the Father has loved me, so have I loved you. Now remain (abide) in my love" (John 15:9). Remaining in His love involves a conscious decision to embrace and cultivate this divine relationship.

God's love is immeasurable and unfathomable, surpassing mere sentiment to become the foundation of our relationship with Him. Abiding in love means allowing this love to saturate every part of our lives, influencing how we see ourselves and relate to others. It's about accepting the full measure of God's love and letting it overflow, touching every individual who crosses our path.

In Ephesians 3:18-21, Paul prays for us to "grasp how wide and long and high and deep is the love of Christ," encouraging us to be filled with the fullness of God. As we reflect on these dimensions of His love, we begin to comprehend its vastness—transforming us from within and inviting us into a deeper journey of abiding.

This profound love is both encompassing and specific. It meets us where we are, amidst life's challenges and joys, offering comfort and strength. When we abide in this love, we find security in an ever-changing world. It becomes the lens through which we view life's circumstances, knowing that there is nothing Christ's love cannot reach, heal, or redeem. As Romans 8:31-39 magnificently assures us, nothing can separate us from the love of God in Christ Jesus.

Reflecting further, 1 Corinthians 13:4-8 outlines love's characteristics—patience, kindness, and truth—guiding our understanding of what it means to love as God loves. This love is enduring and ever-present, prompting us to love from places of strength and vulnerability, courageously extending His grace to others.

Our challenge is to remain consistently rooted in this love, choosing to dwell in it, especially when circumstances might encourage us otherwise. This abiding love requires both receiving it with humility and giving it freely, allowing it to transform everyday life.

Abiding Practice: Gratitude Journal

In today's exploration of abiding in love, let's cultivate gratitude for God's incredible love in our lives.

1. **Find a Quiet Moment**: Set aside a few quiet minutes today to reflect on God's love for you.

2. **Open Your Journal**: Take a notebook or journal where you can write freely about your experience.

3. **Reflect on God's Love**: Think about how His love has been evident in your life. Consider the moments, experiences, or truths that reveal His love to you personally.

4. **Write Three Things You are Grateful For**: Write down three specific things you are grateful for about God's love. These may be broad reflections or specific occurrences where His love was apparent.

5. **Meditate on Each Point**: As you write, pause to meditate on each point. Consider how these aspects of God's love influence your perspective, decisions, and relationships.

6. **Speak a Prayer of Thanks**: Conclude this practice with a heartfelt prayer, thanking God for His unconditional love and asking for His help to remain in it daily.

Let this practice remind you that abiding in God's love is a continual process of receiving and reflecting. By turning your gratitude into an ongoing dialogue, you nurture a heart that thrives in His love, fostering deeper connections with both God and others. As you continue this journal, let it become a testament to the enduring presence of divine love in your life.

WEEK 1: FOUNDATIONS OF ABIDING

Day 3: The Necessity of Abiding

Principle: The Necessity of Abiding

In the whirlwind of contemporary life, where demands are never-ending and distractions abound, the necessity of abiding in Christ becomes all the more essential. Just as a branch cannot thrive without its vine, we are called to remain steadfastly connected to Jesus, our source of life and strength. Without this connection, our spiritual vitality withers, impacting both our inner peace and outward actions.

Jesus emphasizes this crucial truth: "I am the vine; you are the branches. If you remain in me and I in you, you will bear much fruit; apart from me, you can do nothing" (John 15:5, NIV). Abiding in Christ is not a mere suggestion but a vital necessity for experiencing the fullness of life He offers. It's about acknowledging our dependence on Him and choosing each day to draw nourishment from our relationship with our Savior.

The world often tempts us to rely on our own strength and wisdom, promising fulfillment through self-sufficiency. Yet, true fruitfulness—expressed through love, joy, peace, and more—comes solely from remaining in Christ. This necessity calls us out of self-reliance and into a humble posture of dependence, seeking Him in every moment.

As the psalmist declares, "As the deer pants for streams of water, so my soul pants for you, my God" (Psalm 42:1, NIV). This imagery reflects our deep need to abide, to seek His presence, and to be refreshed by His Spirit continually. Abiding is not a one-time event but a daily commitment to lean into God's grace and guidance.

The Apostle Paul reinforces the importance of this continual connection, urging believers in Colossians 2:6-7 (NIV) to "continue to live your lives in him, rooted and built up in him." This rootedness implies a dynamic and ongoing relationship where Christ is our firm foundation, enabling us to grow and thrive spiritually.

When we recognize the necessity of abiding, we find renewed strength to face challenges, wisdom to navigate complexities, and grace to extend to others. Abiding transforms our perspective, helping us to shift from a mindset of striving to one of resting in divine sufficiency. As we remain grounded in God's love and truth, we experience a deeper sense of fulfillment and purpose, touching every facet of our lives.

As Hebrews 4:16 (NIV) invites, "Let us then approach God's throne of grace with confidence, so that we may receive mercy and find grace to help us in our time of need." Our abiding relationship allows us to draw near to God with bold assurance, receiving the sustenance and empowerment required for our journey.

Today, embrace the necessity of abiding. In doing so, you will encounter the enduring power and peace that come from being in constant communion with Christ, discovering that He is truly our all-sufficient source in every circumstance.

Abiding Practice: Morning Prayer

To cultivate this necessity in your life, begin each day with a morning prayer of commitment to abide in Christ.

1. **Choose a Quiet Place**: Designate a peaceful, focused spot where you can start each day, free from distractions. It could be a corner of your room, a comfortable chair, or anywhere that feels calming.

2. **Invite His Presence**: Start your day by inviting Jesus into every moment that lies ahead, acknowledging your need for Him. Allow yourself a few moments to breathe deeply, centering your thoughts on His presence.

3. **Commit to Abide**: Pray a prayer of commitment, expressing your desire to remain connected to Christ throughout the day.

Example Prayer: "Lord Jesus, as I begin this new day, I choose to abide in You. Be my strength and guide, my source of wisdom and love. Help me to stay rooted in Your presence, bearing fruit that reflects Your glory. Amen."

4. **Reflect on Dependency**: Contemplate specific areas where you need God's strength and guidance today. Offer these to Him, trusting in His provision and acknowledging your reliance on His power and grace.

5. **Set an Intention**: Consider a specific intention or focus for the day. It might be a quality like patience, a relationship you wish to nurture, or a challenge you need divine help to face.

6. **Carry the Connection**: Determine to carry the sense of peace and connection from your morning prayer into your entire day. Whenever you find yourself drifting away, take a moment to whisper the prayer again, grounding yourself once more in Him.

Let this morning practice set the tone for your day, establishing a rhythm of reliance and openness to where God is leading you. By recognizing the necessity of abiding, you actively invite Christ into every facet of your life, opening the way for His transformative work to unfold. As you practice this intentional start, may you experience the peace and power that comes from a life deeply connected to the source of all that is good.

WEEK 1: FOUNDATIONS OF ABIDING

Day 4: Abiding over Anxiety

Principle: Abiding over Anxiety

In a world filled with pressures and uncertainties, anxiety can become an unwelcome companion. The complexities of our lives often stir worries that threaten to overshadow our peace and disrupt our connection with Christ. Yet, amidst the storms of anxiety, abiding in Christ offers us a refuge—a place of calm and assurance that transcends our understanding.

Jesus invites us to cast our cares upon Him, reassuring us in Matthew 11:28-30, "Come to me, all you who are weary and burdened, and I will give you rest." This is more than an invitation to find momentary relief; it's a call to dwell continually in His presence, where our burdens are lifted, and our souls are restored.

Paul, in Philippians 4:6-7, exhorts us to turn our anxieties into prayers: "Do not be anxious about anything, but in every situation, by prayer and petition, with thanksgiving, present your requests to God. And the peace of God, which transcends all understanding, will guard your hearts and your minds in Christ Jesus." Here, the necessity of abiding becomes clear; it is our anchor in tumultuous times, a steady presence that wards off anxiety and brings peace.

Abiding in Christ over anxiety means anchoring our hearts in His unchanging love and power, choosing trust over fear. It requires us to replace anxious thoughts with the truths of God's faithfulness, allowing His peace to fill the spaces where worry once resided. This conscious commitment to dwell in His presence transforms our outlook, granting us strength and serenity even when life feels uncertain.

The prophet Isaiah offers a vision of this peace: "You will keep in perfect peace those whose minds are steadfast, because they trust in you" (Isaiah 26:3, NIV). Such peace is not an abstraction but a tangible reality that comes from focusing our minds on the steadfastness of God rather than the instability of our circumstances.

As we learn to abide, we discover that anxiety can be redirected—turned into a prompt that reminds us to return to the security found in Christ's companionship. Embracing this practice reshapes our stress into moments of communion, where we place our cares into hands capable of transforming burdens into blessings.

Abiding over anxiety requires a deliberate shift in posture, from holding onto our worries to surrendering them to God. This surrender is a daily practice, a choice to cultivate a mindset of thanksgiving and petition, inviting God's peace to guard us. As Jesus modeled trust in the Father, even amidst His own trials, we too are invited to rest in God's provision and love.

Today, take the opportunity to abide over anxiety by inviting God into your anxious thoughts. Allow His presence to be your sanctuary, and let His peace guard your heart and mind. Through this abiding relationship, you'll find that the turbulence of anxiety is no match for the calm assurance found in Christ. In Him, we discover the profound truth that peace is not the absence of trouble, but the presence of God.

Abiding Practice: Breath Prayer

Today's practice will help you harness the calming technique of a breath prayer, providing centering moments during stress.

1. **Find a Comfortable Space**: Choose a relaxed spot where you can breathe deeply and focus without interruption. It might be during a break at work, in your car, or at home.

2. **Select a Breath Prayer**: Choose a short, simple prayer that focuses on God's peace and presence. An example might be "God, calm my heart" or "Jesus, bring me peace." Select a phrase that resonates with your need for abiding comfort.

3. **Inhale God's Peace**: As you inhale deeply, silently say the first part of your chosen phrase (e.g., "God"). Imagine breathing in His calmness, peace, and presence.

4. **Exhale Your Worries**: As you exhale slowly, say the second part (e.g., "calm my heart"). Visualize releasing anxiety, tension, and stress, placing them into God's capable hands.

5. **Repeat in Rhythm**: Continue this cycle of breath prayer for several minutes, allowing its rhythm to guide your focus. Let this practice deepen your connection to Christ, acknowledging His presence in your anxious moments.

6. **Invite His Peace**: As you conclude, visualize encapsulating this peace within your heart, carrying it with you through the day's challenges.

Let this breath prayer become a tool in your spiritual arsenal—a practice you can integrate regularly to center yourself in Christ's loving presence. By choosing to abide over anxiety, you invite Jesus into your worries, allowing His peace to reign in your heart and transform your stress into steady assurance. As you embrace this practice, may you find comfort in the knowledge that you are never alone, gently held by the One who calms the storm within and without.

WEEK 1: FOUNDATIONS OF ABIDING

Day 5: Christ as the Vine

Principle: Christ as the Vine

Christ being the vine is not just a metaphor, but a powerful truth that underpins our faith. Jesus stated, "I am the vine; you are the branches" (John 15:5, NIV), emphasizing that He is the essential life-giving source. Everything we are and everything we do flows from our connection with Him. Without Him, we lack the spiritual nourishment needed to thrive.

This imagery calls us to acknowledge the integral relationship between the vine and branches. Just as branches rely on the vine for survival, our spiritual vitality depends on remaining in Christ. He is the source of our strength, wisdom, and renewal—our provider of sustenance, enabling us to grow and bear fruit.

Understanding Christ as the vine means embracing our dependence on Him. It's recognizing that our purpose and potential are found in Him. This abiding relationship offers stability in uncertain times, grounding us in His eternal truth and love. Jesus, as the vine, reminds us of our call to remain in continual communion with Him, which is the foundation of a fruitful life.

Our identity and mission are rooted in this vital connection. As we draw from Him, we become visible expressions of His character to the world—offering love, hope, and life to those around us. Embracing Christ as the vine transforms us, aligning our desires with His purposes, and allowing His life to flow through us into everything we do.

Paul echoes this theme in Galatians 2:20, saying, "I have been crucified with Christ and I no longer live, but Christ lives in me." This reflects the transformation that occurs when we remain connected to Christ; His life becomes evident in ours, influencing how we live and interact with the world.

With Jesus as the vine, we are assured of renewal and growth. In Him, we find empowerment and clarity to live out our calling. Our connection to the vine provides the resources—spiritual, emotional, and intellectual—needed to face life's challenges with resilience and faithfulness.

This interconnectedness invites us to a lifestyle of prayer, reflection, and engagement with Scripture, allowing us to continually draw from His wellspring of life. In doing so, we cultivate a heart attuned to His voice, equipped to discern His will and carry out His work with love.

The invitation is clear: stay connected, draw from His strength, and bear His fruit. In embracing this, we are not only sustained but thrive, becoming conduits of His blessing and transformation in a world in need of hope and renewal. Let us remain in the vine and, through Him, bear much fruit to the glory of God.

Abiding Practice: Visualization

In today's practice, you will use visualization to deepen your understanding of your connection to Christ, the life-giving vine.

1. **Find a Quiet Place**: Choose a peaceful location where you can focus without interruptions. Sit comfortably, close your eyes if it helps you concentrate better, and take several deep breaths to settle your mind and body.

2. **Invite the Holy Spirit**: Begin by inviting the Holy Spirit to guide your thoughts and deepen your connection with Christ during this visualization.

3. **Visualize the Vine and Branches**: Picture in your mind a lush, healthy vine, vibrant and full of life. See yourself as one of the branches, securely connected to this vine. Imagine the strength and life-giving nourishment flowing from the vine into your very being.

4. **Feel the Connection**: Focus on the sensations of this connection. Feel the warmth, energy, and sustenance moving from Christ into you. Consider how this connection supports your spiritual growth and fulfills your purpose.

5. **Reflect on Your Role**: As a branch, understand your role in bearing fruit. What does it mean for you to reflect Christ's character and love in your everyday life? Allow this visualization to remind you of your purpose and potential in Him.

6. **Listen and Rest**: Sit quietly, absorbing the deep connection with Christ. Be open to any insights, impressions, or senses of peace that arise. Rest in the assurance of His continual presence with you.

7. **Prayerful Response**: Conclude with a prayer acknowledging your dependence on Christ as the vine:
"Lord Jesus, thank You for being my life-giving vine. Help me to remain in You, drawing strength and purpose from Your presence. May I bear fruit that glorifies Your name and blesses those around me. Amen."

8. **Carry the Image Forward**: Through your day, return to this image of being connected to the vine whenever you need reassurance or strength. Let it remind you of your unbreakable bond with Christ and His unwavering support.

This practice invites you to explore and deepen your connection with Jesus, the vine, fostering a sense of rootedness and confidence as you navigate your daily life. Let it be a constant reminder of your divine source and the abundant life you have in Him.

WEEK 1: FOUNDATIONS OF ABIDING

Day 6: Detached Without Christ

Principle: Detached Without Christ

The metaphor of the vine and branches in John 15 poignantly illustrates that, apart from Christ, we are like branches cut off from their sustenance. Jesus clarifies this truth: "Apart from me you can do nothing" (John 15:5, NIV). The implication here is profound—the vital connection to Christ is essential for spiritual life, health, and fruitfulness. Without Him, we become detached, losing the flow of divine nourishment that empowers us to thrive and bear fruit.

Detachment from Christ can manifest in various ways: feelings of spiritual dryness, lack of peace or direction, and struggles with purpose or identity. These symptoms signal a need to reconnect, to re-establish our intimate bond with the vine, who is our source of life and strength. Such detachment emphasizes the importance of acknowledging our dependency on Him for sustained spiritual vigor.

In the busyness of life, it's easy to drift away, perhaps without even realizing it, as daily demands, distractions, and self-reliance inch us away from the vine. Yet, recognizing our disconnection is the first step toward renewal. Jesus calls us back to Himself, offering restoration and re-engagement with His life-giving presence.

Abiding in Him invites a conscious realignment—a return to the realization that in Christ we find all we need. It's about acknowledging where we have attempted to produce fruit on our strength and surrendering those areas to the One who makes us whole and fruitful. This process of surrender and reconnection is essential to experiencing the fullness of life that Jesus promises.

Psalm 1:3 offers a vivid contrast to this state of detachment: "That person is like a tree planted by streams of water, which yields its fruit in season and whose leaf does not wither—whatever they do prospers." This imagery reinforces the blessing and vitality that come from staying rooted in our relationship with Christ. When we are nourished by Him, we flourish, demonstrating His vibrant life through our actions and attitudes.

In moments of detachment, let us turn to the promise of Jeremiah 29:13, "You will seek me and find me when you seek me with all your heart." This pursuit of reconnecting with Christ is about seeking Him earnestly, allowing His presence to renew our minds and refresh our spirits.

Apart from Christ, our efforts may falter, leaving us weary and unfulfilled. Yet, His invitation is one of grace, drawing us back into abundant life. As we return to abide in Him, we align our hearts with His will, restoring our peace, reestablishing our sense of purpose, and reigniting our passion for His mission.

Today, reflect on any areas where you feel detached, and invite Christ's renewing presence back into those spaces. Allow His life-giving sustenance to empower you to bear fruit that reflects His love and grace. In Christ, our source, we find the strength and vitality to flourish abundantly, exemplifying His transformative love to the world.

Abiding Practice: Reflection

Today, engage in reflective journaling to identify and surrender areas where you feel disconnected from Christ.

1. **Find a Quiet Place**: Choose a peaceful spot where you can write and reflect without distractions. Take a moment to breathe deeply, inviting the Holy Spirit to guide your thoughts and reflections.

2. **Reflect on Disconnection**: Think about areas in your life where you might feel spiritually disconnected or distant from Christ. It may be a particular situation, an aspect of your personal life, or even a season of doubt or struggle.

3. **Journal Your Thoughts**: Write down any areas where you recognize a lack of connection. Be honest and transparent, knowing that this practice is between you and God.

4. **Examine the Impact**: Consider how this detachment affects your sense of peace, purpose, and fruitfulness. Reflect on how staying connected to Christ could transform these areas.

5. **Surrender Through Prayer**: As you journal, offer these areas to God in prayer. Surrender your struggles, acknowledging your dependence on Him for restoration and guidance.

Example Prayer:
"Lord Jesus, I recognize where I have drifted from You and tried to navigate on my own. Help me to return to You, my true source of life and peace. I surrender [specific areas] to You, trusting in Your love and wisdom to lead me back into full connection. Amen."

6. **Seek His Presence**: Invite Christ's healing presence into these disconnected areas, asking Him to renew and restore your relationship. Allow yourself to rest in His love, knowing He welcomes you back with grace and compassion.

7. **Embrace Renewal**: As you close this reflection, intentionally set your heart on staying connected to Christ. Carry forward the insights and peace you've experienced today, and let them guide you in nurturing your bond with Him.

Through this practice, let today be a turning point—a recommitment to living fully connected to the vine. By acknowledging areas of detachment, inviting Christ's intervention, and leaning into His strength, you'll find renewed engagement and life-giving fruitfulness in your spiritual journey.

WEEK 1: FOUNDATIONS OF ABIDING

Day 7: Abiding through Discipleship

Principle: Abiding through Discipleship

In the journey of faith, discipleship serves as a vital pathway for deeply abiding in Christ. Discipleship involves following Jesus and growing in His likeness through intentional learning and application, often guided by seasoned believers who can provide wisdom and encouragement. This nurturing relationship supports our connection to Christ, reinforcing our growth and transformation.

Jesus' model of discipleship emphasizes community and guidance. During His ministry, He invested in the lives of His disciples, teaching, correcting, and sharing His life with them. In Matthew 28:19-20, His Great Commission instructs us, "Go and make disciples of all nations... teaching them to obey everything I have commanded you." This directive highlights the importance of discipleship as a cornerstone for abiding and growth in Christ.

Abiding through discipleship is about embracing the humility to learn and the courage to teach. It invites us into authentic relationships where we receive and extend wisdom, sharpening and supporting one another. In these interactions, we experience the richness of community, realizing that our faith journey is both personal and communal. The Book of Proverbs reminds us, "As iron sharpens iron, so one man sharpens another" (Proverbs 27:17), emphasizing the transformative potential found in supportive, mentoring relationships.

The communal aspect of discipleship reflects the early church's emphasis on fellowship and learning together. Acts 2:42 tells us they "devoted themselves to the apostles' teaching and to fellowship," underscoring the power of collective spiritual growth. This shared journey strengthens individual faith and fortifies the broader church community.

Connecting with a mentor or trusted guide offers a unique opportunity to explore what abiding means in practical terms. With their support, you can explore challenges, deepen your understanding of Scripture, and integrate spiritual practices into daily life. Their experience and insight become a source of strength, aiding you in navigating the complexities of living a Christ-centered life.

Engaging in discipleship encourages both accountability and encouragement. It is a space where questions can be explored openly, doubts can be expressed honestly, and spiritual practices can be refined. The mentor-mentee relationship symbolizes a journey shared, a dynamic interplay of giving and receiving that nourishes both parties.

As you engage in discipleship, consider how you can both learn from others and impart your understanding to those newer in faith. This cycle of learning and teaching fosters an environment where everyone is spurred on toward deeper maturity in Christ. The commitment to discipleship reflects a dedication to abide in Christ through every season, allowing His influence to permeate both our personal lives and our interactions with those around us.

Today, reflect on the role of discipleship in your faith journey. Reach out to a mentor or seek opportunities to guide others. Let these relationships enrich your understanding and application of abiding in Christ, fostering a community deeply rooted in Him and passionately committed to His mission. Through discipleship, we join a legacy of believers growing in Christ's likeness and extending His love and truth to the world.

Abiding Practice: Connection with a Mentor

Today, take the step of reaching out to a mentor or guide who can walk alongside you in your journey of abiding.

1. **Identify a Mentor**: Reflect on those in your life whose faith you admire. Consider individuals who embody a deep connection with Christ and who offer wisdom and encouragement.

2. **Reach Out for Connection**: Contact this mentor, expressing your desire for connection and support in your journey to abide in Christ. Be open about your intention for spiritual growth and your eagerness for an ongoing conversation.

3. **Discuss Abiding**: Arrange a time to meet or speak, discussing what abiding in Christ means to both of you. Share your reflections and

any areas where you seek guidance or understanding. Listen attentively to their insights and experiences.

4. **Explore Together**: Consider discussing particular challenges or questions you have about abiding. How have they integrated abiding into their own life? What practices or perspectives have they found helpful?

5. **Commit to Ongoing Connection**: If mutually beneficial, propose a plan for regular check-ins or discipleship sessions. This ongoing relationship can become an enduring source of growth and encouragement.

6. **Reflect and Apply**: After your meeting, take time to reflect on what you've learned. Consider ways to apply these insights into your journey of abiding. Document any actionable steps or commitments that arise from the conversation.

7. **Gratitude and Prayer**: Conclude with a prayer of gratitude for your mentor and the opportunity to grow in Christ together. Invite God's wisdom and guidance as you deepen your relationship with Him through discipleship.

Example Prayer:
"Lord, I thank You for the mentors and guides You place in my life. Help me to glean wisdom from their experiences and be open to Your direction through their guidance. May I grow deeper in my abiding relationship with You through this journey. Amen."

Abiding through discipleship enriches your faith journey, anchoring you in Christ's love and truth. By engaging in this practice, you not only build a stronger foundation in your own life but also open channels for mutual growth and support. Embrace the gift of community and mentorship as vital parts of your quest to abide deeply in Christ.

WEEK 1: FOUNDATIONS OF ABIDING: SMALL GROUP DISCUSSION GUIDE

Ice Breaker:

- "Share one highlight from your week that helped you feel connected to God."

Scripture Reading: John 15:1-11

- Invite someone to read the verses aloud.
- Reflect on how the imagery of the vine and branches speaks to the necessity of remaining in Christ.

Discussion Questions:

1. **Abiding as Connection:**
   - What insights did you gain from the quiet reflection practice on John 15:4-5?
   - How does viewing oneself as a branch connected to Jesus change your perspective on daily life and spirituality?

2. **Abiding in Love:**
   - How did writing in your gratitude journal impact your understanding of God's love this week?
   - In what ways can we allow God's love to transform our interactions with others?

3. **The Necessity of Abiding:**
   - How did your morning prayer practice influence your perspective on your need for Jesus throughout the day?
   - Can anyone share a moment when they felt the necessity of abiding during a challenging time this week?

4. **Abiding over Anxiety:**

- How did you find the breath prayer practice in times of anxiety or stress?
- What areas of life do you feel most challenged to replace anxiety with trust in God?

5. **Christ as the Vine:**
    - In what ways did the visualization exercise help you feel more connected to Christ?
    - How do you see your role in bearing fruit as part of God's kingdom?

6. **Detached Without Christ:**
    - What did you discover about areas where you may feel spiritually disconnected?
    - How can the group support you as you seek to reconnect with Christ?

7. **Abiding through Discipleship:**
    - How was your experience in connecting with a mentor or guide?
    - What insights or encouragement did you gain from this interaction?

Application & Action:

- Reflect on one principle from Week 1 that you want to continue focusing on as we move into the next week.
- How can the group help you maintain your commitment to this practice?

Prayer:

- Spend a few moments in open prayer, inviting participants to share any prayer requests related to abiding in Christ or personal challenges.

- Close with a group prayer, thanking God for His presence and asking for guidance as everyone continues this journey of abiding.

Closing Thought:

- Encourage each participant to keep a spirit of openness to God's work in their daily life, allowing His presence to transform ordinary moments into opportunities for spiritual growth and connection.

WEEK 2: ABIDING IN PRACTICE

Day 8: Abiding in the Word

Principle: Abiding in the Word

Abiding in Christ finds one of its richest expressions through engaging deeply with His Word. Scripture serves as both a guide and a wellspring of life, illuminating our path and reshaping our hearts and minds. Psalm 119:105 reminds us, "Your word is a lamp for my feet, a light on my path." Immersing ourselves in the Word is essential for nurturing a profound connection with Jesus.

The Bible is not merely a collection of historical texts but the living and active voice of God. As we read and reflect on scripture, we encounter God's character, His promises, and His will for our lives. This abiding through the Word strengthens our foundation, equipping us with wisdom, encouragement, and discernment to face life's challenges. Hebrews 4:12 affirms this, saying, "For the word of God is alive and active. Sharper than any double-edged sword, it penetrates even to dividing soul and spirit, joints and marrow; it judges the thoughts and attitudes of the heart."

Engaging with scripture cultivates intimacy with God. As we meditate and memorize His Word, it becomes etched in our hearts, transforming our thoughts and actions. Jesus, in His wilderness temptation, demonstrated the power of scripture memorization, using specific verses to counter temptation (Matthew 4:1-11). Abiding in God's Word provides both strength and guidance, helping us align our lives with His divine purposes.

By internalizing scripture, we allow God's truths to permeate every aspect of our being. It becomes a source of comfort in trials, a guidepost for decision-making, and a reservoir of joy that sustains us through all seasons. Joshua 1:8 speaks to the importance of this practice: "Keep this Book of the Law always on your lips; meditate on it day and night, so that you may be careful to do everything written in it. Then you will be prosperous and successful."

Abiding in the Word is not a passive endeavor, but an active engagement that draws us deeper into the heart of God. It invites us into a dialogue where we listen for His voice and respond with openness and receptivity.

In John 15:7, Jesus promises, "If you remain in me and my words remain in you, ask whatever you wish, and it will be done for you." This abiding relationship, rooted in Scripture, fosters a faith that is both dynamic and resilient, poised to impact not only our lives but the lives of those around us.

Today, make a conscious decision to engage more intentionally with God's Word. Establish a rhythm of reading, reflecting, and praying through scripture, allowing its truths to shape you. Consider how you can incorporate practices like journaling, group study, or scripture memorization to deepen your engagement. Through this abiding in the Word, discover the rich, sustaining connection with God that guides you with grace and speaks His truth into every corner of your life.

Abiding Practice: Scripture Memorization

Today, deepen your abiding relationship by committing a key verse of scripture to memory.

1. **Select a Verse**: Choose a verse that resonates with your current journey. It might be a line of encouragement, a promise you hold dear, or a truth you want to anchor in your heart.

Suggested verses:

- Psalm 46:1-11 (God is our refuge & strength)
- Proverbs 4:20-27 (guarding your heart)
- James 1:1-15 (trials & temptation)
- James 1:19-27 (hearing & doing the Word)
- Galatians 5:16-26 (walking in the Spirit)
- 1 Timothy 4:6-16 (serving Christ)
- Colossians 3:12-25 (family relationships)
- John 3:14-18 (salvation)
- 1 Peter 5:5-11 (humility, anxiety, suffering)
- Ephesians 6:10-18 (spiritual warfare, prayer)
- Ephesians 4:20-32 (Christian life)
- Psalm 139:1-15 (God made you and knows you)
- Psalm 119:9-16 (memorizing God's Word)
- Romans 12:9-21 (Christian life)
- 2 Timothy 3:14-17 (value of Scripture)
- Philippians 4:4-13 (contentment)

- 1 Thessalonians 5:12-22 (life lessons)
- Lamentations 3:21-26 (God's mercy & goodness)
- Psalm 119:97-105 (God's Word directs)
- Psalm 19 (God's Word is perfect)
- Titus 3:3-8 (salvation)
- Genesis 1:26-31 (creation mandate)
- Matthew 22:34-40 (greatest commandment)
- Philippians 2:1-11 (humility, mind of Christ)
- Colossians 1:15-20 (character of Christ)
- 1 John 4:7-18 (God is love)
- Proverbs 3:5-12 (trust in the Lord)

2. **Write it Down**: Write the verse on a card, piece of paper, or in your journal. Writing it out helps start the imprinting process on your memory and allows for easy reference.

3. **Break It Down**: Divide the verse into manageable parts or phrases. Focus on memorizing each section thoroughly before moving onto the next. Repeat this process until you can recite the entire verse from memory.

4. **Engage All Senses**: Speak the verse aloud as you memorize it, engaging both your visual and auditory senses. Consider visualizing the imagery or message within the verse, allowing it to connect deeply with your heart and mind.

5. **Reflect on Meaning**: Spend time meditating on the verse's meaning, considering how it applies to your life. What is God revealing to you through this scripture? How does it guide or encourage you?

6. **Review and Revisit**: Throughout the day, repeat the verse during quiet moments or as challenges arise. Revisit it consistently throughout the week, seeing it becomes an integral part of your thought processes.

7. **Prayerful Commitment**: Conclude by asking God to embed this verse deeply in your heart, enabling you to live and abide more fully in His truth.

Example Prayer:
"Heavenly Father, thank You for the gift of Your Word. Help me to internalize and live out this verse, drawing strength and wisdom from its truth. May it remind me to remain in You and guide me in my daily walk. Amen."

This practice of scripture memorization not only strengthens your memory, but it fosters a heart that remains open to God's voice. As you engrain His Word into your being, it transforms your thoughts, attitudes, and actions, deepening your connection with Christ. Let this verse become a daily companion, leading you to abide richly in the life-giving love of Jesus.

WEEK 2: ABIDING IN PRACTICE

Day 9: Abiding in Prayer

Principle: Abiding in Prayer

Prayer is the lifeline of our abiding relationship with Christ—a means of maintaining continuous, open communication with God. Through prayer, we align our hearts with His will, find comfort in His presence, and draw strength from His unending grace. Jesus modeled this constant connection, withdrawing to pray and communicate with the Father even amidst His demanding ministry (Luke 5:16).

Abiding in prayer is about more than bringing our requests to God; it's about cultivating a conversation that deepens over time, thereby strengthening our relationship with Him. It serves as a place where we express our gratitude, seek wisdom, and intercede for others. In prayer, we become more attuned to the Spirit's leading, gaining clarity and direction for our lives. This dynamic exchange invites us to listen actively and speak honestly, fostering a genuine dialogue with the Divine.

This disciplined pursuit fosters a posture of dependence and surrender, inviting God into every aspect of our lives. Philippians 4:6-7 reminds us that through prayer, "the peace of God, which transcends all understanding, will guard your hearts and your minds in Christ Jesus." This peace stems from knowing we can approach God with our praises and burdens alike. Through prayer, our anxieties find release, and our hearts open to receive God's enduring peace and assurances.

Jesus taught His disciples to pray with simplicity and faith, exemplified in the Lord's Prayer (Matthew 6:9-13). This model highlights essential components of prayer: adoration, supplication, confession, and submission to God's will. It encourages us to approach God as our loving Father, entrusting Him with our needs and desires, while seeking alignment with His kingdom purposes.

Establishing fixed prayer times throughout the day helps anchor us in this rhythm of abiding, creating intentional moments to pause, reflect, and reconnect with God. This practice encourages consistency, ensuring that the noise of life does not overshadow the voice of our Savior. Daniel's example in Daniel 6:10 illustrates the power of regular prayer, as he faithfully prayed three times a day despite facing persecution.

We are encouraged to approach God with the openness that He modeled during Gethsemane—a place of raw honesty and earnest seeking. Through prayer, we cultivate a reliance on God's strength and perspective, allowing His wisdom to guide us through life's uncertainties and decisions.

Today, choose to deepen your practice of prayer. Set aside moments to intentionally connect with God, free from distractions. Consider how you can incorporate prayer into your routine—whether through structured times, spontaneous moments, or a mix of both. As you do, let prayer become the steady heartbeat of your relationship with Christ, nurturing your soul and equipping you for a life lived in tune with His grace and truth. Through this abiding practice, may you experience the fullness of His presence and the unwavering peace that surpasses all understanding.

Abiding Practice: Set Daily Prayer Times

Today, develop a habit of abiding in prayer by scheduling fixed times for prayer throughout your day.

1. **Choose Your Prayer Times**: Identify moments that best suit your daily rhythm. Consider incorporating prayer into natural breaks or transitions, such as upon waking, before meals, during a lunch break, and before bedtime. Aim for at least three set times.

2. **Create a Prayer Space**: Designate a quiet spot for prayer in each setting—at home, work, or wherever you find yourself. Having a familiar space can enhance focus and consistency.

3. **Set Reminders**: Use alarms or notifications to remind you of your prayer times. This acts as a gentle nudge, encouraging you to prioritize abiding in God's presence.

4. **Prepare to Engage**: As the time approaches, center your heart and mind on God. Take a moment to breathe deeply, clearing away distractions and opening yourself to His voice.

5. **Offer a Balanced Prayer**: During each prayer time, aim to include:

- Praise and gratitude: Acknowledge God's goodness and give thanks for His blessings.
- Confession and surrender: Reflect on any struggles or burdens, placing them in God's hands.
- Intercession: Pray for the needs of others, lifting up friends, family, or global concerns.
- Guidance and listening: Invite the Holy Spirit to guide you, sitting in silence to hear God's whisper.

6. **Journal Your Experience**: If time allows, jot down any thoughts, impressions, or scripture that may surface during prayer. This helps track your journey and reveals God's faithfulness over time.

7. **Live in Continuous Prayer**: Between your designated times, cultivate an attitude of prayerfulness by inviting God into everyday moments and decisions. Let His presence accompany you throughout your day.

Example Prayer:
"Lord, as I come to You in prayer, I open my heart to receive Your wisdom, peace, and guidance. Anchor me in Your love and help me to listen attentively to Your voice. May my day reflect the depth of my connection with You. Amen."

Establishing set prayer times disciplines your life into a pattern of staying connected with Christ. As you prioritize these moments, the focus and peace they bring invite you to abide more fully in Him, enriching your walk and reinforcing your trust in His unwavering presence.

WEEK 2: ABIDING IN PRACTICE

Day 10: Abiding in Community

Principle: Abiding in Community

Abiding in Christ is not a journey we undertake alone; it thrives in the rich context of community. Together with other believers, we experience the fullness of life Christ intends for us, supporting and sharpening one another in faith and love. Hebrews 10:24-25 urges us, "not giving up meeting together, as some are in the habit of doing, but encouraging one another—and all the more as you see the Day approaching."

Community provides spaces where we can grow, learn, and hold one another accountable. In fellowship, we practice bearing one another's burdens, celebrating joys, and exploring the depths of God's Word together. These shared experiences deepen our relationship with Christ, as we witness His love and grace manifested in collective harmony. Proverbs 27:17 reminds us, "As iron sharpens iron, so one person sharpens another," highlighting the transformative power of nurturing relationships grounded in Christ.

Through gathering, we mirror Jesus' priorities. Throughout His ministry, He drew people together, emphasizing the importance of community and shared mission. Jesus often surrounded Himself with His disciples, teaching and encouraging them. He demonstrated the beauty of communal living and working together toward a common purpose, exemplified in John 13:34-35, where He commands, "Love one another. As I have loved you, so you must love one another."

Authentically engaging with others embodies the Gospel's call to love and serve, uniting hearts and minds in Christ's name. This engagement reflects the early church's example found in Acts 2:42, which notes they "devoted themselves to the apostles' teaching and to fellowship, to the breaking of bread and to prayer." These gatherings were marked by shared lives and active participation in each other's spiritual journeys.

Participating in a small group or fellowship nurtures this abiding sense, offering opportunities for mutual encouragement and growth. It's within these close-knit gatherings that insights deepen, faith solidifies, and the communal aspect of abiding flourishes. These groups become sanctuaries of truth and grace, where believers can openly share their triumphs and trials, finding support and understanding.

Community also offers accountability, helping us stay aligned with God's truth and encouraging us to live out our faith authentically. It allows us to serve one another through spiritual gifts, providing practical expressions of Christ's love and fostering an environment where everyone contributes to the body of Christ.

Today, reflect on how you can embrace the community in your journey of abiding. Seek to actively engage with fellow believers, whether through a weekly worship service, small group, or fellowship event. Allow these connections to deepen your faith and broaden your understanding of God's work in the world. Together, as a community rooted in Christ, may we reflect His love and grace, transforming our lives and the lives of those around us. Through these shared experiences, we journey toward the fullness of life found in Christ.

Abiding Practice: Gathering with Believers

Today, commit to experiencing the richness of abiding by connecting with a community of believers.

1. **Find a Group or Fellowship**: Reach out to your church to join a small group, fellowship, or Bible study that aligns with your interests and schedule. If you're seeking a community, consider exploring local churches.

2. **Engage Actively**: Attend the meeting with an open heart and mind. Be prepared to both give and receive, contributing your unique perspective and encouraging others on their journey.

3. **Share and Listen**: During the gathering, be authentic in sharing your experiences, thoughts, and questions. Listen attentively to others, valuing their insights and stories.

4. **Explore Scripture Together**: Participate in scriptural reflection and discussions. Allow group study to deepen your understanding and appreciation of God's Word, exploring how it applies to your collective experiences.

5. **Encourage One Another**: Intentionally offer words of encouragement and support to your fellow believers. Look for ways you can pray for and uplift each other in your spiritual journeys.

6. **Reflect on the Experience**: After the gathering, take time to reflect on what you learned and how it impacts your faith. Note any insights or commitments to apply as you continue to abide.

7. **Cultivate Community**: Commit to regular participation, nurturing relationships and maintaining consistent connection. Consider extending hospitality to your group by opening your home for fellowship or organizing an outing.

Example Prayer:
"Heavenly Father, thank You for the gift of community and for the fellowship of believers. Help me engage fully with my group, learning and growing in Your love. May our gathering reflect Your kingdom and inspire us to live out our faith boldly. Amen."

By participating in community gatherings, you allow the beauty of fellowship to enrich your journey, strengthening your relationship with Christ and others. Through the shared bond of faith, we become vessels of divine love and grace, carrying His presence into the wider world around us. Let this practice encourage you to abide in the fullness of life that's possible when we walk alongside fellow believers.

WEEK 2: ABIDING IN PRACTICE

Day 11: Abiding in Worship

Principle: Abiding in Worship

Worship is a vital expression of our abiding relationship with God. It's more than just a Sunday service; it's a lifestyle that reveres and honors God in all we do. Worship invites us to focus our hearts and minds on Christ, celebrating His greatness and deepening our connection with Him. In John 4:23-24, Jesus speaks of true worshipers who worship "in spirit and in truth," emphasizing genuine, heartfelt devotion over ritualistic practices.

Abiding in worship means consistently inviting God's presence into everyday moments, allowing our hearts to overflow in adoration, gratitude, and praise. This practice aligns us with God's will, re-centers our priorities, and energizes our spirit, transforming routine experiences into sacred moments. Romans 12:1 exhorts us to offer our bodies as living sacrifices, illustrating that worship encompasses every aspect of our lives, turning ordinary actions into opportunities to honor God.

Personal worship through music offers a powerful avenue to connect with God intimately. Music has the unique ability to express our deepest emotions, bridging the gap between our hearts and heaven. Whether through singing, playing an instrument, or simply listening, worship through music ushers us into a space of reflection, surrender, and awe. The Psalms, often set to music, are filled with examples of worship that express longing, thankfulness, and reverence, connecting us deeply with the heart of God.

By setting aside intentional time for personal worship, we cultivate an environment where God's presence is magnified, allowing us to align our lives with His truth and experience His transformative power. This devoted practice opens our hearts to receive God's love and direction, forging a path for His peace and joy to permeate our daily experiences.

Furthermore, collective worship in community serves as a powerful expression of unity and shared faith. Gathering with others to worship forms a bond that strengthens and encourages, allowing us to experience

God through the collective voices and hearts of His people. It moments that we glimpse the beauty of God's diverse family together in a common purpose, amplifying our individual exp faith.

As you embark on the journey of abiding in worship, consider how you can incorporate both personal and communal worship into your routine. Create space for moments of reflection and praise, inviting God's presence into every facet of life. Whether in stillness or exuberance, worship is the expression of our love for God, drawing us nearer to His heart and aligning us with His purpose.

Today, let worship be both your anchor and your expression, a reminder of who God is and how deeply He loves you. Engage in worship with sincerity and passion, transforming each encounter with God into an opportunity for growth and renewal. As you worship in spirit and truth, experience the depth of God's love and faithfulness, and discover the joy of a life lived in continual reflection of His glory.

Abiding Practice: Personal Worship

Today, embrace the practice of personal worship through music to enrich your abiding relationship with God.

1. **Set Aside Time**: Allocate a specific time each day for personal worship. This could be in the morning to start your day, during a lunch break for renewal, or in the evening to wind down.

2. **Create a Worship Space**: Designate a spot conducive to worship. It might be a comfortable chair, a room with good acoustics, or a quiet corner where you can focus fully on God.

3. **Choose Worship Music**: Select worship songs or playlists that resonate with your heart and current journey. These might include hymns, contemporary worship, or instrumental music that elevates your spirit.

4. **Engage Fully**: As you play or sing the music, engage your heart, mind, and soul. Allow the lyrics and melodies to guide your thoughts toward God's love and presence. Use this time to express adoration, gratitude, and surrender.

5. **Be Open to the Spirit**: Invite the Holy Spirit to move during your worship time. Be receptive to His prompting and open to receiving insights, comfort, or encouragement.

6. **Reflect and Respond**: After your worship, take a moment to reflect on how God spoke to you and how you feel. Consider writing down any thoughts, feelings, or revelations that emerged during your worship.

7. **Integrate Worship into Daily Life**: Let the heart of worship carry throughout your day. Return to this space of adoration in everyday moments, offering praise to God in conversations, work, and leisure.

Example Prayer:
"Lord, I come before You in worship, offering my heart and spirit in adoration. May this time of music draw me closer to You and deepen my connection with Your presence. Fill my soul with Your peace and guidance. Amen."

By engaging in personal worship through music, you open your heart to God's presence, nurturing your abiding relationship with Him. Let this practice become a source of renewal and inspiration, transforming each day into a testimony of His grace and unfolding His love in your life. As you dwell in worship, may you encounter the fullness of His joy and peace, reflecting His light to the world around you.

WEEK 2: ABIDING IN PRACTICE

Day 12: Abiding with the Spirit

Principle: Abiding with the Spirit

Abiding with the Holy Spirit brings richness to our relationship with God, offering us wisdom, guidance, and the assurance of His continual presence. Jesus promised His followers a Helper, the Holy Spirit, who would teach, remind, and comfort us in all things (John 14:26, NIV). This divine companionship allows us to navigate life with discernment and clarity, grounded in the confidence that we are never alone.

When we remain open to the Spirit's leading, we invite God's perspective into our hearts and minds. Abiding with the Spirit means cultivating an attitude of attentiveness and allowing Him to direct our steps, both big and small. This practice embraces a posture of humility, where we acknowledge our dependence on God's wisdom over our limited understanding. Proverbs 3:5-6 underscores this principle, urging us to "trust in the Lord with all your heart and lean not on your own understanding."

Listening for the Spirit's guidance goes beyond speaking in prayer; it involves creating space for silence, where the whispers of God can be heard. In a world filled with noise, this intentional pause cultivates receptivity, helping us discern His guidance in both the mundane and profound aspects of life. Romans 8:26 reminds us that "the Spirit helps us in our weakness," interceding for us and aligning our hearts with God's will.

The relationship with the Holy Spirit also includes embracing His gifts and fruit in our lives. As we abide, we are invited to participate in the Spirit's work, cultivating virtues such as love, joy, peace, patience, kindness, and self-control (Galatians 5:22-23). This fruit not only reflects our growing relationship with God but also serves as an authentic witness to others.

By embracing the Holy Spirit's active presence, we deepen our connection with God, experiencing His transforming power and love in our present journey. This connection is dynamic and life-giving, empowering us to act with courage, speak with wisdom, and love with divine compassion. He equips us to face challenges with strength and grace, carrying the assurance that God Himself is guiding and sustaining us.

Today, invite the Holy Spirit into every part of your life, moment by moment. Practice his presence by actively listening and responding to His guidance. Seek to cultivate an environment where the Spirit's voice can be heard and His influence can be felt. As you embrace this divine companionship, discover the richness of a life aligned with God's purposes, and experience the profound peace and joy that comes from walking closely with His Spirit. Through this relationship, may you find strength and fullness, transforming your journey into a testimony of God's abiding presence.

Abiding Practice: Listening for Guidance

Today, focus on the practice of listening for the Holy Spirit's guidance by spending intentional time in silence after prayer.

1. **Prepare Your Heart**: Before you begin, quiet yourself with deep breaths, inviting the Holy Spirit to fill your heart and mind. Set the intention to remain open and receptive to what God may reveal.

2. **Offer a Simple Prayer**: Start by offering a sincere prayer inviting God's presence and guidance. Express your desire to hear and follow His will.

Example Prayer:
"Holy Spirit, I invite You into this time of stillness. Open my heart to Your voice and guide me with wisdom and love. I am here to listen and learn. Amen."

3. **Enter a Time of Silence**: Set a timer for five minutes to focus solely on listening. Resist the urge to fill the silence with words or thoughts, embracing this opportunity to be fully present. Let go of any distractions or concerns you may have, trusting the Spirit to guide you.

4. **Be Attentive to Impressions**: As you sit in silence, pay attention to any insights, impressions, or thoughts that arise. Allow yourself to be aware of the subtle nudge of the Spirit, without forcing any specific outcome.

5. **Embrace Peace and Openness**: Allow the quiet to envelop you, inviting the peace that comes from resting in the presence of the Holy Spirit. Trust in His perfect timing and guidance, even if clarity doesn't come immediately.

6. **Reflect and Respond**: After the silent period, take a moment to reflect on any thoughts or impressions that emerged. Consider writing them in a journal, along with any feelings or commitments that arise. Let this reflection guide your actions and decisions throughout the day.

7. **Integrate Listening into Daily Life**: Encourage a habit of listening for the Spirit's guidance beyond structured times of silence. Develop an awareness of His presence in everyday situations, inviting His wisdom in conversations, decisions, and challenges.

Example Intention:
"Lord, throughout today, help me remain attuned to Your voice, discerning Your guidance with clarity and trust. Allow my steps to align with Your purpose. Amen."

By dedicating time to listening for the Spirit, you nurture a sensitive heart ready to receive His wisdom and love. As you cultivate this practice, embrace the peace and assurance of God's faithful presence, allowing it to shape your journey and influence your world for His glory.

WEEK 2: ABIDING IN PRACTICE

Day 13: Abiding Amid Busyness

Principle: Abiding amid Busyness

In our fast-paced world, busyness can often overshadow our ability to abide in Christ. The constant presence of notifications and information can fragment our attention, making it challenging to maintain a deep connection with God. Yet, even amid the clamor, Christ invites us to rest in Him, to find peace and presence amid the noise.

Jesus modeled a balanced life of engagement and retreat, consistently taking time to step away from crowds to be alone with the Father. Mark 6:31 reminds us of Jesus' invitation to His disciples: "Come with me by yourselves to a quiet place and get some rest." This practice of retreating allowed Him to replenish His spirit and realign with God's will, preparing Him for His ministry. His example encourages us to integrate moments of solitude and reflection into our daily lives, finding renewal and focus.

Abiding amid busyness requires intentionality—setting boundaries that protect our focus and priorities. One practical way to cultivate this is through a "Digital Sabbath," a period intentionally set aside to disconnect from electronic devices, allowing space to engage with God and loved ones without distraction. This intentional practice provides an opportunity to step back from the digital world and into the tangible presence of God, enhancing our awareness of His closeness.

By creating this intentional margin, we invite moments of stillness to hear God's whisper and refuel our spirit. As Psalm 46:10 urges, "Be still, and know that I am God." This pause helps us reconnect with the essence of our faith, nurturing our souls and bringing clarity and peace amid life's demands.

In taking these intentional steps, we affirm that our identity and worth are not defined by digital engagement but by the presence of our loving Creator. It's a reminder that even amidst life's hustle, we can prioritize what truly matters—our connection with God and our relationships with those around us.

Today, explore how you can implement practices like a Digital Sabbath to foster deeper abiding. Consider making space regularly where you can disconnect from technology and reconnect with God. Embrace the peace and purpose that come from aligning your spirit with His, and let this rhythm of rest and engagement renew your heart and mind. Through these conscious choices, find a steadiness that transcends the world's chaos and centers you in the abiding love and grace of God.

Abiding Practice: Digital Sabbath

Today, experience the peace of abiding by taking a Digital Sabbath—intentionally disconnecting from electronics for a set period.

1. **Choose Your Sabbath Time**: Decide on a specific time period for your Digital Sabbath. This might be an entire day, a few hours during an afternoon, or an evening before bed. Select the duration that best fits your schedule and needs.

2. **Set Boundaries**: Communicate your intentions to those who might be affected, explaining your plan to disconnect for this period. Set any necessary boundaries to help protect this time, enabling you to focus without interruption.

3. **Plan Activities**: Identify alternative activities to engage in during your Digital Sabbath. These could include reading, journaling, prayer, spending time in nature, engaging in creative pursuits, or sharing quality time with family or friends.

4. **Create a Sacred Space**: Designate a restful environment that supports your intention to unplug. Remove or silence electronics and physical distractions, substituting them with items that bring peace, such as candles, books, or inspiring music.

5. **Enter into Rest**: As you begin your Digital Sabbath, center yourself with prayer, inviting God to fill the space with His presence and peace. Open your heart to hear Him uniquely during this time.

Example Prayer:
"Lord, as I disconnect from distractions, draw me closer to You. Help me to rest in Your presence, embracing the simple joys and moments of stillness. May this Sabbath refresh and renew my spirit. Amen."

6. **Embrace the Experience**: Engage fully with your chosen activities, allowing yourself to unwind and be present. Notice how stepping aside from technology fosters a deeper sense of connection and awareness of God's presence.

7. **Reflect and Relate**: At the end of your Sabbath, take a few moments to reflect on your experience. Journal any insights or feelings that arose during this time. Consider how this practice fed your soul and ways you might incorporate ongoing Sabbaths into your life.

Example Reflection:
"Thank You, Lord, for the peace and clarity I found in Your presence. As I resume my daily activities, help me carry this sense of rest and connection, remaining open to Your voice and leading. Amen."

Through the practice of a Digital Sabbath, you create sacred moments that prioritize abiding amid busyness. As you cultivate this rhythm, discover the beauty and depth of engaging with God intentionally, finding rest, renewal, and abiding peace in His presence. Let this intentional pause remind you of the value of connecting with Christ and others, enriching both your journey and daily life.

WEEK 2: ABIDING IN PRACTICE

Day 14: Abiding through Obedience

Principle: Abiding through Obedience

Abiding in Christ naturally leads us toward a life of obedience—aligning our actions with His will and reflecting His love through our deeds. Obedience is not about rigid compliance, but a heartfelt response to God's love and guidance, an outward expression of our inward commitment. Jesus underscores this truth: "If you love me, keep my commands" (John 14:15, NIV), highlighting the intrinsic relationship between love and obedience in our walk with Him.

Obedience involves consciously choosing God's ways over our desires, allowing the Holy Spirit to transform and guide us. It's about the small and large decisions that align our lives with God's character and purposes. Through obedience, we participate in God's work, becoming conduits of His love, grace, and redemption to the world. This act of submission is grounded in trust, acknowledging that God's ways are higher than ours and lead to true joy and fulfillment.

Performing acts of kindness embodies this obedient lifestyle, reflecting Christ's compassion in tangible ways. Jesus exemplified kindness through His ministry, reaching out to the marginalized, healing the sick, and offering forgiveness. As we follow His example, we abide through obedience—practicing kindness as an intentional, loving response to the needs of those around us.

James 1:22 calls us to be "doers of the word, and not hearers only," inviting us to translate our faith into action. When we act with kindness, we demonstrate a living faith, one that not only hears the Word but embodies it through deeds that testify to God's unending mercy and love.

Obediently aligning with Christ's teachings cultivates a life rich with purpose and fulfillment. It invites us into a divine partnership, where our obedience allows God to work through us, impacting the world with His truth and light. This collaboration draws us into a deeper understanding of His heart and reinforces our abiding connection.

Today, reflect on how your life can exemplify obedience through acts of kindness. Recognize opportunities to extend God's love to those around you, whether through simple gestures or significant commitments. Let this obedience be a source of joy and freedom, as you experience the blessing of being in step with His will. Through abiding obedience, may you illuminate the path with God's love, becoming a true reflection of the grace and compassion of Christ to everyone you encounter.

Abiding Practice: Act of Kindness

Today, deepen your abiding relationship by intentionally performing an act of kindness for someone else.

1. **Open Your Heart**: Begin by setting your intention through prayer. Ask God to open your eyes to opportunities to serve and reflect His love through acts of kindness.

Example Prayer:
"Lord, guide me to see the needs around me and give me the courage to serve others with a loving heart. May my actions reflect Your grace and compassion, drawing others closer to You. Amen."

2. **Identify an Opportunity**: Look for someone in your life—whether a friend, family member, colleague, or stranger—who might benefit from a kind gesture. Seek the Holy Spirit's guidance in identifying their needs, approaching each opportunity with sensitivity and open-mindedness.

3. **Choose an Act of Kindness**: Decide on a specific act that reflects Christ-like love. This could be offering a listening ear, writing a thoughtful note, helping with a task, providing a meal, or giving a heartfelt compliment.

4. **Perform with Intentionality**: As you carry out your act of kindness, focus on the intention behind it—an expression of your love for God and others. Engage with presence and sincerity, trusting that even small gestures can make a significant impact.

5. **Reflect on the Experience**: Afterward, spend a few moments reflecting on the impact of your kindness. How did it affect the recipient and yourself? Consider journaling your thoughts and how this practice brings you closer to abiding in obedience.

6. **Seek Ongoing Opportunities**: Cultivate a lifestyle of kindness by seeking additional opportunities to extend love and serve others. Allow this practice to shape your interactions, echoing Christ's love wherever you go.

7. **Conclude with Prayer**: Offer a prayer of gratitude for the privilege of serving others, asking God to continue to guide your heart toward obedience in all aspects of life.

Example Prayer:
"Thank You, Lord, for the opportunity to reflect Your love through kindness. May my life be a testament to Your grace, continually seeking to abide in obedience. Guide my heart to serve with sincerity and joy. Amen."

By intentionally performing acts of kindness, you express your love for God through obedience, abiding in His presence as you extend His compassion to others. Let this practice become a natural extension of your walk with Christ, deepening your connection with Him and inspiring those around you to experience His love and grace.

WEEK 2: ABIDING IN PRACTICE: SMALL GROUP DISCUSSION GUIDE

Ice Breaker:

- "Share one small blessing or moment of gratitude from your week. How did it make you feel more connected to God?"

Scripture Reading: Psalm 119:105

- Invite someone to read the verse aloud.
- Reflect on how God's Word illuminates your path and how it shapes your spiritual journey.

Discussion Questions:

1. **Abiding in the Word**:
    - How did the practice of Scripture memorization impact your week?
    - What verse did you choose to memorize, and why is it significant to you?

2. **Abiding in Prayer**:
    - How did setting daily prayer times affect your connection with God this week?
    - What challenges or insights did you experience during your prayer times?

3. **Abiding in Community**:
    - How did engaging with a community of believers enrich your experience of abiding?
    - What stood out to you during your group fellowship or Bible study?

4. **Abiding in Worship**:
    - How did personal worship through music transform your spiritual journey this week?

- What songs or worship experiences drew you closer to God?

5. **Abiding with the Spirit**:
    - What insights did you gain from practicing silent listening for the Spirit's guidance?
    - How can you continue to foster attentiveness to God's voice in everyday life?

6. **Abiding amid Busyness**:
    - Share your experience of the Digital Sabbath. How did disconnecting impact your sense of connection with God and others?
    - What practices can help you balance technology use with spiritual presence moving forward?

7. **Abiding through Obedience**:
    - How did performing an act of kindness reinforce your understanding of obedience as a form of abiding?
    - How can we encourage each other to live out acts of kindness consistently?

Application & Action:

- Reflect on a principle from Week 2 that deeply resonated with you. How can you integrate this practice into your ongoing daily life?
- How can the group support you as you continue to practice abiding in these ways?

Prayer:

- Invite participants to share prayer requests related to their experiences with the week's practices and any ongoing challenges.
- Close with a group prayer, inviting the Holy Spirit to solidify the week's learning and guide each member toward deeper, more intentional abiding.

Closing Thought:

- Remind group members that the journey of abiding is ongoing, and every small step taken in faith and community is a step toward deeper intimacy with Christ. Encourage each person to allow God's word, prayer, fellowship, and actions to continually transform their everyday lives.

WEEK 3: DEEPENING THE ABIDING

Day 15: Abiding through Reflection

Principle: Abiding through Reflection

Reflection is an essential component of deepening our abiding relationship with God. It involves taking intentional time to pause and consider how God is moving and present in our lives. Through reflection, we gain insight into His guidance, recognize His hand at work, and cultivate a heart of gratitude and awareness. Psalm 77:11-12 instructs us, "I will remember the deeds of the Lord; yes, I will remember your miracles of long ago. I will consider all your works and meditate on all your mighty deeds."

Abiding through reflection allows us to process our experiences through the lens of God's love and truth, reinforcing our connection with Him. It heightens our awareness of His presence, enabling us to align more closely with His purposes. By regularly reflecting on God's activity, we learn to walk with greater faith and discernment. This awareness transforms our perspective, allowing us to see both trials and triumphs as part of His redemptive work in our lives.

Throughout His ministry, Jesus often withdrew to solitary places to reflect and pray, seeking renewed focus and connection with the Father (Matthew 14:23). This rhythm provides a model for us, inviting moments of stillness to remember and realign with God's presence. Such intentional pauses allow us to lay aside the busyness of life and listen for His still, small voice, bringing clarity and peace amid chaos.

Engaging in evening reflection offers a structured opportunity to review the day with Christ, appreciating both the joys and challenges and inviting His insight and peace as we move forward. This practice can involve journaling about your experiences, expressing gratitude for God's blessings, and seeking understanding for the lessons in difficult moments. It is an opportunity to thank God for His faithfulness and to entrust tomorrow into His hands.

Reflection also encourages us to take stock of how our actions and attitudes align with God's will. By contemplating our choices and responses, we are better able to adjust and recalibrate to reflect Christ more accurately in all we do. This ongoing practice of review and realignment is an essential aspect of spiritual growth, fostering a humble, teachable spirit.

Today, dedicate time to engage in intentional reflection. Invite God to reveal His perspective on your daily experiences, and allow His presence to illuminate the path forward. As you cultivate this discipline, watch as your relationship with God deepens, your awareness of His activity sharpens, and your journey of faith becomes more attuned to His leading. Abiding through reflection transforms moments of stillness into sources of strength, guiding you into a fuller, richer life in Christ.

Abiding Practice: Evening Reflection

Today, embrace evening reflection as a way to deepen your abiding connection with God by reviewing the day's experiences in His presence.

1. **Set Time for Reflection**: Choose a quiet moment near the end of your day for undisturbed reflection. Create a peaceful environment—perhaps with soft lighting or gentle music—to foster contemplation.

2. **Begin with Prayer**: Invite God's presence and guidance as you reflect on the day. Ask the Holy Spirit to illuminate moments of His activity and help you recognize His guidance and provision.

Example Prayer:
"Heavenly Father, thank You for this day and for being with me through each moment. As I reflect on how You have moved today, open my heart to see Your presence and learn from Your guidance. Amen."

3. **Review Your Day**: Silently recall key events, interactions, and experiences from the day. Consider how God was present in each moment—whether through blessings, challenges, or lessons learned.

4. **Identify God's Movement**: Reflect on specific moments when you sensed God's presence or guidance. What insights did you gain? How did God provide strength, wisdom, or encouragement?

5. **Express Gratitude**: Acknowledge and give thanks for God's provision and presence throughout your day. Offer gratitude for the growth and blessings He brought into your experiences.

6. **Seek Learning and Growth**: Consider any areas where you struggled or felt distant from God. What can you learn from these moments? How might you invite His presence and strength into similar situations in the future?

7. **Conclude with Peace**: End your reflection with prayer, seeking God's peace for the night and renewal for the next day. Surrender any lingering concerns to Him, trusting in His faithfulness and love.

Example Prayer:
"Lord, thank You for the ways You have been present today. As I rest, fill me with Your peace. Help me carry the lessons and gratitude into tomorrow, abiding in Your love and wisdom. Amen."

By dedicating time for evening reflection, you cultivate a rhythm of continual connection with God, deepening your awareness of His presence in your life. Let this practice become a peaceful and insightful end to your day, nurturing your abiding relationship and preparing your heart for what God has in store.

WEEK 3: DEEPENING THE ABIDING

Day 16: Abiding through Trials

Principle: Abiding through Trials

Trials and challenges are inevitable parts of life, but they also offer profound opportunities for deeper abiding in Christ. Through these difficulties, we are invited to lean more heavily on His strength, grace, and wisdom, allowing Him to shape our character and deepen our faith. James 1:2-4 encourages us: "Consider it pure joy, my brothers and sisters, whenever you face trials of many kinds, because you know that the testing of your faith produces perseverance. Let perseverance finish its work so that you may be mature and complete, not lacking anything."

Abiding through trials means embracing the process of surrender, acknowledging our limitations, and trusting God's ability to carry us through. It involves releasing our worries and relying on His presence, knowing that He works all things for our good (Romans 8:28). In surrendering our burdens to God, we open our hearts to His peace and allow Him to refine us, turning challenges into opportunities for growth and transformation.

Jesus, in His moments of trial, modeled surrender through prayer in the Garden of Gethsemane. Even as He faced incredible hardship, He sought connection with the Father, saying, "Not my will, but yours be done" (Luke 22:42). This posture of surrender provides a powerful example of abiding trust and reliance on God's plan. It shows us that even in our darkest moments, we can lean on God, trusting Him to guide us through and ultimately bring about His perfect will.

When confronted with life's trials, abiding in Christ requires us to shift our focus from our circumstances to the One who holds us. It calls us to stand firm in our faith, trusting that God's grace is sufficient, even when we feel weak. As 2 Corinthians 12:9 reassures us, "My grace is sufficient for you, for my power is made perfect in weakness." Through our trials, God's strength becomes evident, and His power shines through our vulnerability.

Abiding through trials includes gratitude for God's presence and purpose. While challenges can be painful, they are also moments when God draws us closer, teaching us to rely on Him for sustenance and wisdom. By maintaining an attitude of gratitude, we recognize His providence in every situation, cultivating a heart that remains open to His blessings, no matter the circumstance.

In facing trials, reflect on how your faith can be strengthened through surrender. Align your thoughts and actions with God's promises, seeking His guidance in prayer and Scripture. Invite Him to use your challenges as a canvas for His transformation, shaping you into His likeness. As you abide through trials, find comfort in knowing that God's love is steadfast and that He walks with you every step of the way.

Embrace the refining process that trials offer, allowing them to deepen your connection with Christ and fortify your faith. Through these experiences, you will discover a greater capacity for resilience and a profound understanding of God's peace, empowering you to live boldly and trustfully in His provision.

Abiding Practice: Surrender Prayer

Today, practice surrendering your worries and trials to God through a dedicated Surrender Prayer.

1. **Find a Quiet Place**: Choose a comfortable and peaceful location where you can focus on prayer without distractions. Take a moment to breathe deeply, inviting God's presence into this time of surrender.

2. **Center Yourself in God's Presence**: Begin by acknowledging God's sovereignty and love. Remind yourself of His promises to be with you through every trial and challenge.

3. **Identify Your Worries and Trials**: Take a few minutes to reflect on specific worries or trials you are currently facing. Name them silently or write them down, allowing yourself to become aware of their weight.

4. **Offer a Surrender Prayer**: As you bring each concern before God, practice releasing it into His hands. Invite Him to take control and seek His guidance through full surrender.

Example Prayer:
"Lord, You know the burdens I carry. I surrender [specific worries/trials] to You now, trusting in Your power and wisdom. Help me to find peace in Your presence and the courage to face each day with faith. Let Your will be done in my life. Amen."

5. **Embrace God's Peace**: After surrendering your worries, sit quietly, allowing God's peace to fill your spirit. Envision His love enveloping you, bringing rest and assurance, even amid challenges.

6. **Reflect on Surrender**: Spend a few moments considering how surrender impacts your heart and mind. How does relinquishing control to God change your perspective on your trials? What areas might you need to continually surrender to maintain this peace?

7. **Invite Continuous Surrender**: Conclude by inviting God to guide you in daily surrender. Commit to returning to this practice whenever worries threaten to overwhelm, trusting Him to carry you through.

Example Reflection:
"Lord, thank You for embracing my worries and trials with Your love. As I walk this path, remind me to lean on You, surrendering each burden into Your trustworthy hands. May my faith grow through this journey, abiding in Your strength always. Amen."

By practicing a Surrender Prayer, you cultivate the habit of relying on God through trials, deepening your abiding relationship in both trust and reliance. Let this practice guide you in navigating challenges with peace and resilience, as you experience God's presence and faithfulness in every step of your journey.

WEEK 3: DEEPENING THE ABIDING

Day 17: Abiding and Simplicity

Principle: Abiding and Simplicity

Simplicity is a spiritual discipline that aligns us more closely with God's presence and purposes. In a world filled with distractions, clutter, and complexity, embracing simplicity helps us focus on what truly matters—our relationship with Christ. Abiding in simplicity means shedding the excess that can cloud our spiritual vision and embracing a lifestyle that prioritizes our connection with God.

Jesus exemplified a life of simplicity, often teaching through parables that emphasized the value of trusting God for our needs and the dangers of being entangled by material possessions. Luke 12:15 reminds us, "Then he said to them, 'Watch out! Be on your guard against all kinds of greed; life does not consist in an abundance of possessions.'" His teachings invite us to examine our lives critically, discerning what truly brings fulfillment and joy.

Abiding in simplicity encourages us to evaluate the priorities that shape our daily lives. By letting go of what distracts us from God, we create space for His voice and His presence. This spiritual decluttering brings clarity, allowing us to focus on building a rich, meaningful relationship with Him. Simplicity is not about deprivation but about making intentional choices that reflect our desire to seek first the Kingdom of God (Matthew 6:33).

By simplifying our external and internal lives, we make room for deeper abiding, allowing God more space to work within us. This spiritual clarity helps us discern God's voice and directs our actions towards His kingdom purposes. Paul writes in 1 Timothy 6:6, "But godliness with contentment is great gain," reflecting the beauty of leading a life rooted in divine purpose rather than worldly excess.

The practice of decluttering can serve as a tangible expression of this principle. Simplifying a space in your home or an area of your life can foster peace and intentionality, creating a physical reflection of the internal order and focus we strive to maintain. As you simplify, consider what possessions or commitments serve your spiritual growth and which ones detract from it.

Furthermore, simplicity impacts our mental and emotional well-being. By intentionally reducing the noise and chaos of life, we cultivate a peaceful environment conducive to prayer and meditation. This simplicity allows us to rest in God's presence, free from the pressures of maintaining unnecessary complexity.

As you embrace simplicity, reflect on how this discipline can transform your daily life. Consider what changes you can make to align your lifestyle more closely with your spiritual values. Whether it's decluttering a room, reducing commitments, or simplifying your schedule, each step toward simplicity strengthens your ability to abide with Christ.

Today, invite God to guide you in this journey of simplicity. Ask Him to illuminate areas that need realignment and to grant you the courage to make choices that foster a closer connection with Him. Through this discipline, experience the freedom and peace that come from prioritizing what truly matters—your abiding relationship with God.

Abiding Practice: Declutter

Today, embrace the discipline of simplicity by decluttering an area of your life or a space in your home.

1. **Identify an Area**: Choose a specific area to declutter, whether a physical space like a room, closet, desk, or a life aspect, such as your schedule or digital presence. Consider where simplifying could create more peace or focus in your life.

2. **Set an Intention**: Before you begin, set an intention for this practice. Pray for guidance, seeking to honor God through simplicity and inviting His presence into this space.

Example Prayer:
"Lord, help me embrace simplicity as a way to draw closer to You. Guide my heart and hands as I declutter, removing what distracts and hinder my connection with You. Let this practice open space for Your peace and purpose. Amen."

3. **Begin the Declutter**: Start sorting through items with discernment, asking yourself if they serve a purpose or bring joy. Let go of what no longer aligns with your priorities or God's leading in your life.

4. **Reflect on the Process**: As you work, reflect on what this decluttering represents in your spiritual journey. Consider how simplifying your surroundings or life choices might facilitate a deeper connection with Christ.

5. **Create a Restful Space**: Once decluttered, arrange the area to encourage peace and create opportunities for rest, reflection, or prayer. Allow the simplified space to inspire clarity and calm.

6. **Practice Gratitude**: Conclude by expressing gratitude for the freedom and clarity gained through simplicity. Acknowledge God's role in helping you create this space.

Example Reflection:
"Thank You, Lord, for the clarity and peace found in simplicity. As I create space, help me to focus on the things that truly matter, nurturing my relationship with You. May this practice reflect my commitment to living a life centered on Your love and grace. Amen."

7. **Seek Ongoing Simplification**: Consider how you might extend this practice of simplicity to other areas of your life, implementing rhythms that consistently reflect your commitment to abiding fully in God.

By decluttering, you engage with the discipline of simplicity, creating tangible expressions of your desire to abide deeply in Christ. Let this practice encourage a lifestyle that prioritizes connection over clutter, fostering peace, focus, and a deeper walk with your Savior.

WEEK 3: DEEPENING THE ABIDING

Day 18: Abiding through Service

Principle: Abiding through Service

Service is a powerful expression of abiding in Christ. As we remain connected to Him, His love naturally flows through us, compelling us to reach out and serve others. Jesus modeled a life of service, teaching that true greatness is found in serving and uplifting those around us. In Matthew 20:28, Jesus states, "Just as the Son of Man did not come to be served, but to serve, and to give his life as a ransom for many."

Abiding through service allows us to embody the love and compassion of Christ, building bridges and transforming lives through tangible acts of kindness. It shifts our focus outward, reminding us that our faith is not only about personal growth but also about impacting the world for the betterment of others. This selfless nature of service aligns us more closely with God's purposes, deepening our relationship with Him, as reflected in Galatians 5:13, which encourages us to "serve one another humbly in love."

Service is more than an activity; it's a lifestyle that reflects Christ's heart. Through volunteering, we engage with our communities and contribute to their flourishing. Acts of service demonstrate God's love in action, offering hope and support to those in need. In serving, we often find our true purpose and fulfillment, experiencing God's presence in the act of giving, for it is more blessed to give than to receive (Acts 20:35).

When we serve, we embody the principle of Philippians 2:3-4: "Do nothing out of selfish ambition or vain conceit. Rather, in humility value others above yourselves, not looking to your own interests but each of you to the interests of the others." This perspective transforms our understanding of service into an opportunity to uplift others and share the light of Christ.

Service also serves as a substantial witness to the Gospel. When we sacrificially serve others, we reflect the heart of Christ to the world, providing a living testimony of God's gracious love and mercy. Through acts of kindness, we draw people closer to Him, planting seeds of faith that can lead to transformation and renewal.

Engaging in service activities fosters community and builds lasting relationships. Whether through organized efforts or simple, spontaneous acts of kindness, each opportunity to serve enriches our lives and those we encounter. It reminds us that we are interconnected and that our actions can create ripples of positivity and hope.

Today, consider how you can incorporate service into your daily life. Look for opportunities to volunteer in your community, support those in need, or simply perform random acts of kindness. As you serve, invite God to work through you, trusting that He will use your efforts to uplift and inspire.

Let service be a continuous outpouring of your abiding relationship with Christ, a reflection of His love and compassion in every interaction. Through this commitment, discover the joy and fulfillment that arise from living a life dedicated to serving others, embodying the essence of Christ in action.

Abiding Practice: Volunteer

Today, deepen your abiding relationship by serving others through volunteer work.

1. **Research Local Organizations**: Explore opportunities to volunteer with local organizations that align with your interests or causes you're passionate about. Consider charities, community groups, food banks, shelters, or faith-based initiatives.

2. **Pray for Guidance**: Begin with prayer, seeking God's guidance on where He wants you to serve. Ask for an open heart to discern His direction and to serve wholeheartedly.

Example Prayer:
"Lord, guide me to opportunities where I can serve others and reflect Your love. Show me where my gifts and passions can meet the needs of those around me. May my service be an offering to You, revealing Your grace in action. Amen."

3. **Reach Out**: Contact organizations to learn about their volunteer needs and how you can contribute. Sign up for a role that resonates with you and commits time to participate.

4. **Serve with Intention**: As you volunteer, approach your service with intentionality and joy. Be present, engaging genuinely with those you serve and fellow volunteers. Allow Christ's love to shine through your actions and interactions.

5. **Reflect on the Experience**: After serving, reflect on your experience. Consider how serving impacted both you and the community. How did it enhance your understanding of abiding in Christ? Write down any insights or lessons learned.

6. **Commit to Regular Service**: Consider making volunteering a regular part of your life. Look for ongoing opportunities to serve and incorporate this practice as a rhythm of your faith journey.

7. **Conclude with Gratitude**: Offer thanks for the chance to serve and the ways God worked through you. Acknowledge His presence and the connections made through your service.

Example Reflection:
"Thank You, Lord, for the privilege of serving others. As I offer my time and efforts, let me always abide in Your love, seeing each act as a way to glorify You. Deepen my connection with You and others through service, and continue to guide me in making an impact. Amen."

By volunteering, you embrace the principle of abiding through service, allowing the love of Christ to extend beyond yourself into your community. Let this practice remind you of the joy and fulfillment found in serving others, fostering a deeper connection with God and the world around you.

WEEK 3: DEEPENING THE ABIDING

Day 19: Abiding in God's Promises

Principle: Abiding in God's Promises

God's promises are an unshakeable foundation for our faith and a vital source of hope and encouragement. They remind us of His faithfulness, goodness, and commitment to us. Abiding in these promises means actively holding onto and applying them in our lives, letting them shape our perspectives and actions.

Scripture is filled with declarations of God's intentions and assurances for His people. Joshua 23:14 declares, "You know with all your heart and soul that not one of all the good promises the Lord your God gave you has failed." This affirmation invites us to trust fully in God's Word, leaning on His promises through life's various seasons. It speaks to the reliability and steadfast nature of God's Word, encouraging us to rely on His truth even in the face of uncertainty.

By embracing His promises, we anchor our hearts in truth, strengthening our resilience and perspective during challenges. God's promises remind us of His presence in every situation, guiding us to live with faith and assurance rather than fear and doubt. They become lenses through which we view our circumstances, offering peace and confidence rooted in God's unchanging nature.

The practice of documenting these promises allows us to remember and meditate on them consistently. By recording God's promises, we create a personal testimony of His ongoing faithfulness and discover fresh strength and encouragement in our daily walk with Him. Writing them down in a journal, annotating Bible verses, or placing reminders where we can easily see them helps reinforce God's assurances in our minds and hearts.

Psalm 119:148, "My eyes stay open through the watches of the night, that I may meditate on your promises," highlights the power of constant reflection on God's Word. This meditation invites us to internalize His promises and let them seep into every corner of our lives, bringing stability and calmness amid chaos.

Additionally, sharing God's promises with others can be an

encouragement not only for ourselves but for the community we are part of. Speaking these truths over one another builds corporate faith and collective resilience, reinforcing the truth that God's Word is alive and active in all our lives.

As you focus on God's promises, reflect on how they speak into your current situations. Consider which promises are particularly relevant for you today and how they can bolster your faith. In moments of doubt or difficulty, turn to His Word as a reminder of His unending commitment to you.

Today, embrace the transformative power of God's promises. Allow them to shape your interactions, decisions, and outlook. Through them, find reassurance and strength, resting in the steadfast hope that God's promises never fail. As you do, let these truths propel you into deeper trust and vibrant faith, evidenced by peace and joy that permeate every aspect of life.

Abiding Practice: Promise Journal

Today, deepen your abiding relationship by starting a Promise Journal, noting down God's promises discovered in Scripture.

1. **Select a Journal**: Choose a journal or notebook dedicated to recording God's promises. This will become a personal, cherished resource of encouragement.

2. **Read Scripture Intentionally**: As you read the Bible, pay special attention to verses or passages that highlight God's promises. Reflect on how these promises speak to your current season or circumstances.

3. **Record the Promises**: Write down the promises you encounter, noting the reference and any personal reflections or insights. Consider exploring the context to understand how they relate to God's character and assurances.

Example Entry:
"Promise: 'I am with you always.' (Matthew 28:20)
Reflection: In moments when I feel alone, this promise reminds me I'm never alone. God's presence is my constant companion, offering peace

and guidance."

4. **Meditate and Pray**: Spend time meditating on these promises, allowing them to permeate your heart. Pray them back to God, thanking Him for His faithfulness and asking for the grace to trust in them each day.

5. **Reflect on the Impact**: Consider how abiding in God's promises affects your thoughts, feelings, and decisions. How do they encourage and empower you to live confidently in His will?

6. **Revisit Often**: Regularly return to your Promise Journal, especially during times of challenge or uncertainty. Let it be a wellspring of hope and assurance, reminding you of God's unchanging character and love.

7. **Share and Encourage**: Consider sharing a promise that has impacted you with others. Use your journal to bless and encourage friends, family, or your faith community with the truths you've discovered.

Example Prayer:
"Lord, thank You for the promises woven throughout Your Word. Help me to internalize these truths and rely on them daily. Open my heart to Your steady assurance, letting Your promises guide and sustain me. Amen."

By engaging in a Promise Journal, you nurture an intentional habit of abiding in God's assurances. Let this practice infuse your daily life with hope and trust, allowing His promises to be a constant source of encouragement, drawing you closer to Him in faith and confidence.

WEEK 3: DEEPENING THE ABIDING

Day 20: Abiding with Humility

Principle: Abiding with Humility

Humility is foundational to our relationship with God, acknowledging our imperfections and our reliance on His grace. Abiding with humility means recognizing our need for Him and approaching His presence with a posture of surrender and openness. James 4:10 encourages us, "Humble yourselves before the Lord, and he will lift you up." This deep humility draws us closer to God, allowing His strength to work through our weaknesses.

Confession is a powerful practice that embodies humility, inviting us to present our failings and sins before God, seeking His forgiveness and renewal. It's not just about acknowledging our mistakes but recognizing our dependence on God's grace and mercy. Through confession, we experience the freedom of letting go of burdens and the joy of being embraced by His absolution. 1 John 1:9 assures us, "If we confess our sins, he is faithful and just and will forgive us our sins and purify us from all unrighteousness."

This act of confession renews our hearts, creating a clear path for God's transformative work and drawing us into deeper fellowship. By regularly practicing humility through confession, we refresh our spiritual walk, maintaining a humble spirit that eagerly receives God's ongoing sanctification.

Jesus exemplified humility throughout His life, modeling it in servanthood and surrender, culminating in His sacrificial death. In Philippians 2:7-8, we read about Jesus' humility in taking human form and obedience to the cross—His life an invitation for us to embrace humility in our abiding walk. Jesus' actions teach us that true greatness is found not in exalting ourselves, but in serving others and submitting to God's will.

Embracing humility also means acknowledging that we don't have all the answers and being open to God's guidance and the wisdom of others. This openness fosters a growth mindset, where we learn from our experiences and remain teachable, allowing the Holy Spirit to lead us in truth and love.

In relationships, humility fosters empathy and understanding, encouraging us to consider others' perspectives and needs. By valuing others and putting them before ourselves, we strengthen community bonds and reflect Christ's love in our interactions. Romans 12:16 advises, "Live in harmony with one another. Do not be proud, but be willing to associate with people of low position."

Today, let humility guide your walk with Christ. Reflect on areas where pride might hinder your relationship with Him or others, and seek His wisdom and strength to embrace a humble heart. Engage in confession and open your heart to God's transforming grace, allowing Him to renew and lift you.

Through humility, may you find deeper connection and alignment with God, drawing strength from His presence and grace. As you embody the humility of Christ, let your life testimony of His love and mercy, inviting others to experience His generous and forgiving heart.

Abiding Practice: Confession

Today, deepen your abiding relationship with God through the practice of confession, allowing yourself to be transformed by His grace.

1. **Find a Quiet and Reflective Space**: Choose a tranquil setting where you can openly communicate with God. Take a moment to still your mind and heart, inviting the Holy Spirit's presence into this sacred time.

2. **Acknowledge God's Holiness**: Begin by acknowledging God's holiness and perfection. Reflect on His righteousness and love, setting the tone for your time of confession.

3. **Reflect on Your Heart and Actions**: Spend a few moments examining your heart and actions. Identify areas where you've fallen short—whether in thoughts, words, or deeds. Ask the Holy Spirit to reveal anything that needs to be confessed and surrendered to God.

4. **Offer Your Confession**: Humbly present your sins and shortcomings to God, expressing genuine sorrow and a desire for

renewal. Speak or write specific confessions, trusting in God's promise of forgiveness.

Example Confession:
"Lord, I come before You with humility, acknowledging where I've fallen short. I confess [specific sin/struggle] and ask for Your forgiveness. Help me to turn from these ways and draw closer to Your will. Amen."

5. **Receive God's Grace**: After confessing, sit in quiet reflection, allowing yourself to receive God's grace and forgiveness. Envision His love washing over you, bringing healing and acceptance. Let His grace fill you with peace and renewed strength.

6. **Commit to Growth**: Reflect on how you can align your life more closely with God's ways moving forward. Consider steps to foster growth and prevent recurring patterns, relying on the Spirit for guidance.

7. **Conclude with Thanksgiving**: End your time of confession with gratitude for God's mercy and transformative power. Acknowledge His constant love and grace, committing to carry this assurance into your daily walk.

Example Prayer:
"Thank You, Lord, for Your forgiveness and love. As I rest in Your grace, help my heart to remain humble, seeking to abide with You in truth and righteousness. Guide my steps, and may my life reflect Your love and mercy. Amen."

By engaging in confession, you embrace humility before God, allowing His grace to transform your heart and align you more closely with His purposes. Let this practice enhance your abiding relationship, fostering a deeper sense of peace and reliance on His boundless love and forgiveness.

WEEK 3: DEEPENING THE ABIDING

Day 21: Abiding through Rest

Principle: Abiding through Rest

Rest is an essential rhythm woven into the fabric of our spiritual lives, reflecting God's own model of work and rest. Abiding through rest means taking intentional time to cease from our labors, allowing space for spiritual renewal, physical restoration, and deeper connection with God. Psalm 46:10 invites us to "Be still, and know that I am God," calling us into stillness where we can experience His presence and peace.

Sabbath rest is a gift, an opportunity to focus not on productivity but on being with God and finding replenishment in His presence. Through rest, we honor the rhythm God established at creation and that Jesus exemplified throughout His ministry, where He consistently withdrew to be alone with the Father (Mark 6:31). This intentional withdrawal serves as a reminder that our worth is not determined by our work, but by our relationship with God.

This practice cultivates an abiding awareness of our dependence on God and the sufficiency of His provision. By setting aside time for Sabbath, we prioritize our relationship with God over the demands of daily life, fostering a spirit of thankfulness and contentment. During these moments of rest, we allow ourselves to reflect on God's goodness, renew our strength, and realign our priorities with His will.

Rest also serves as a powerful antidote to the hustle and stress of modern life, offering a sacred pause that refocuses and recharges us. It provides the margin needed to hear God's voice amidst the noise, preparing us for the work He calls us to do. As Isaiah 30:15 reminds us, "In returning and rest you shall be saved; in quietness and in trust shall be your strength."

Embracing rest, however, requires intentionality. In a culture that often equates busyness with success, choosing to rest can be countercultural but deeply rewarding. It invites us to trust that God will sustain us and that His grace is sufficient for all our needs.

To integrate rest into your spiritual rhythm, consider setting specific times for Sabbath each week—a day or even a few hours dedicated to unplugging from work and responsibilities. Use this time to engage in activities that nourish your soul and draw you closer to God, such as prayer, worship, reading, or spending time in nature. Let this restful time become a renewal of your spirit, refreshing your heart and mind.

Today, reflect on the role of rest in your life and how it can enhance your abiding relationship with God. Allow rest to be not just a cessation of work, but a sacred practice that nurtures your spiritual growth and deepens your connection with your Creator. Through rest, experience the fullness of God's presence and the peace that transcends all understanding, equipping you to live out your calling with grace and purpose.

Abiding Practice: Sabbath Rest

Today, embrace the principle of abiding through rest by dedicating a day or set period to Sabbath rest and renewal.

1. **Choose a Sabbath Time**: Decide on a day or portion of a day to dedicate to rest. This can be a full day or several hours, depending on your schedule and commitments.

2. **Prepare Your Heart and Mind**: Approach this time with intention, setting aside responsibilities and distractions. Pray for a spirit open to experiencing God's rest and renewal.

Example Prayer:
"Lord, as I enter this time of Sabbath rest, help me to lay down my burdens and focus on Your presence. Fill my heart with peace and refresh my spirit, drawing me closer to You. Amen."

3. **Plan Activities for Renewal**: Identify activities that nourish your soul and foster connection with God and loved ones. Consider reading, prayer, time in nature, creativity, or enjoying a meal with family or friends.

4. **Create a Restful Environment**: Set the atmosphere in your home or chosen space to encourage relaxation and tranquility. Consider soft lighting, calm music, or even turning off electronics to promote stillness.

5. **Spend Time in Spiritual Reflection**: Use part of your Sabbath for reflection and prayer, meditating on Scripture or journaling. Open your heart to God's voice, seeking His guidance and reassurance.

6. **Embrace Community and Joy**: If possible, spend some of your Sabbath time in community, sharing meaningful interactions with those who inspire joy and connection. Allow these relationships to renew and uplift you.

7. **Conclude with Gratitude**: As your Sabbath concludes, give thanks to God for this time of rest and express your appreciation for His presence and renewal. Reflect on how this period has deepened your abiding relationship and encouraged your spirit.

Example Reflection:
"Thank You, Lord, for the gift of Sabbath rest. May this time of renewal fill me with Your peace and align me with Your purposes. As I return to my daily routine, help me carry the spirit of rest and gratitude in my heart. Amen."

By dedicating time to Sabbath rest, you honor the rhythm God designed for your life, embracing moments of stillness and renewal that deepen your abiding relationship with Him. Let this practice strengthen your connection with the Creator, bringing balance, peace, and joy to your everyday journey.

WEEK 3: DEEPENING THE ABIDING: SMALL GROUP DISCUSSION GUIDE

Ice Breaker:

- "Share about a time this week when you felt God's presence. What was happening around you, and how did it impact your day?"

Scripture Reading: Psalm 77:11-12

- Invite someone to read the verses aloud.
- Reflect on the significance of remembering God's deeds and meditating on His works.

Discussion Questions:

1. **Abiding through Reflection**:
    - How did the practice of evening reflection impact your perception of God's presence throughout the day?
    - What specific insights or experiences stood out to you during your moments of reflection?

2. **Abiding through Trials**:
    - How did engaging in the Surrender Prayer help you navigate any challenges this week?
    - Can you share a trial where you felt God was teaching or transforming you?

3. **Abiding and Simplicity**:
    - Describe your experience with the decluttering exercise. How did it affect your sense of peace and space for God?
    - How might simplicity in various areas of life open up more room for spiritual growth?

4. **Abiding through Service**:

- What was your experience like during the volunteer activity? How did it reinforce the concept of abiding through service?
- How can we cultivate a lifestyle of service that continuously reflects our relationship with Christ?

5. **Abiding in God's Promises:**
    - How did creating a Promise Journal influence your trust in God's faithfulness? *Psalm 23*
    - What promise did you find most impactful, and how does it apply to your current season of life?

6. **Abiding with Humility:**
    - In what ways did the practice of confession enhance your sense of humility and reliance on God's grace?
    - What steps can we take to maintain humility in our daily walk with God? *2 Chron 7:14*

7. **Abiding through Rest:**
    - Share the insights gained during your Sabbath rest. How did this time refresh your spirit and connect you more deeply to God?
    - How can we build regular Sabbath practices into our lives for ongoing renewal?

Application & Action:

- Reflect on a specific practice from Week 3 that you found transformative. How can this practice become a regular part of your spiritual routine?
- How can the group support one another in maintaining these practices and deepening the abiding journey together?

Prayer:

- Invite participants to share prayer requests related to their experiences with the week's practices and any personal challenges.

- Close with a group prayer, thanking God for His faithfulness and asking for continued growth and guidance as participants seek to deepen their abiding relationship with Christ.

Closing Thought:

- Encourage group members to keep pursuing intimacy with God through reflection, simplicity, service, and rest. Remind them that their journey of abiding leads them into greater depths of God's love and provision, enriching their lives and those around them.

WEEK 4: TRANSFORMATIVE ABIDING

Day 22: Abiding and Transformation

Principle: Abiding and Transformation

Abiding in Christ naturally leads to transformation—a continual process of becoming more like Him in heart, mind, and spirit. As we remain connected to Jesus, the Holy Spirit works within us, refining our character and guiding us toward growth and maturity. 2 Corinthians 3:18 captures this journey: "And we all, who with unveiled faces contemplate the Lord's glory, are being transformed into his image with ever-increasing glory, which comes from the Lord, who is the Spirit."

Transformation is not a one-time event but an ongoing process that unfolds as we surrender ourselves to God's will. It involves embracing change as a vital part of our spiritual journey, allowing God to prune and shape us according to His purposes. This process is a testament to God's redemptive work, inviting us to live fully in His grace and truth. As we are transformed, our lives become increasingly reflective of Christ's love and holiness, radiating His light to the world.

By asking God to reveal areas where we need to grow, we open ourselves to the depth and beauty of His transformative power. This willingness to change demonstrates a heart that is responsive to the Spirit's leading, eager to align more closely with God's vision for our lives. Such openness requires humility and faith, trusting in God's goodness to guide us through the challenges and joys of transformation.

Philippians 1:6 reassures us that "He who began a good work in you will carry it on to completion until the day of Christ Jesus." This assurance reminds us that God's commitment to our growth is unwavering; He is faithfully working within us, even when progress feels slow or imperceptible. Our transformation is held in His capable hands.

Transformation through abiding also involves the renewal of our minds and hearts. Romans 12:2 exhorts us to "be transformed by the renewing of your mind," inviting us to adopt a perspective shaped by God's truths rather than worldly influences. This renewal equips us to discern God's will and live out His good, pleasing, and perfect plan for our lives.

As we grow in Christlikeness, our relationships reflect this ongoing change. We develop greater capacity for love, patience, forgiveness, and kindness, fostering deeper connections with others and displaying the power of God's work within us. Our lives become living testimonies of His grace and transformative power.

Today, reflect on areas where God may be calling you to experience transformation. Invite the Holy Spirit to illuminate aspects of your life that need change and be open to His guidance. Trust that as you abide in Christ, He will faithfully work in you, bringing you into closer alignment with His image and purpose.

Embrace this journey of transformation, knowing that God's grace is sufficient and His love is unending. Through abiding in Him, become a vessel of His glory, radiating His presence and allowing His transformative power to impact the world around you.

Abiding Practice: Invite Change

Today, invite God to transform you by asking Him to reveal areas for growth and development.

1. **Create a Quiet Space**: Find a peaceful location where you can focus and pray without interruptions. Allow this environment to foster openness and receptivity.

2. **Open Your Heart in Prayer**: Begin by inviting the Holy Spirit to illuminate areas in your life where God desires to bring transformation. Ask for clarity and courage to embrace the changes He reveals.

Example Prayer:
"Heavenly Father, I invite You to search my heart and show me areas where I need to grow and change. Open my eyes to Your vision for my life, and grant me the strength and willingness to follow Your leading. Amen."

3. **Reflect on Your Life**: Spend time reflecting on different aspects of your life—emotions, relationships, habits, and priorities. Consider where you feel God nudging you toward growth or new directions.

4. **Listen for God's Guidance**: Sit in silence, allowing time for the Holy Spirit to speak. Be attentive to any thoughts, impressions, or prompts that arise. Trust in God's gentle guidance and love.

5. **Identify Areas for Transformation**: Note specific areas where you sense God calling you to change. Whether in attitudes, behaviors, or spiritual practices, acknowledge your need for His help to become more like Christ.

6. **Commit to Growth**: Prayerfully consider steps you can take to invite transformation in these areas. Set intentions or goals, and lean on God's strength to support you in this journey.

7. **Thank God for His Work**: Conclude by thanking God for His faithfulness and the transformative work He is doing in your life. Express your trust in His plans and your commitment to walking in His ways.

Example Reflection and Prayer:
"Lord, thank You for revealing areas where You desire change in my life. As I step forward with faith, help me stay rooted in Your love and truth. May my life increasingly reflect Your image, bringing glory to Your name. Amen."

By inviting God to lead you toward transformation, you open yourself to the ongoing work of His Spirit, allowing His love and power to reshape your life. Let this practice encourage a heart responsive to God's presence, fostering growth and reflecting His grace to all those around you.

WEEK 4: TRANSFORMATIVE ABIDING

Day 23: Abiding in Mission

Principle: Abiding in Mission

Abiding in Christ compels us to engage in His mission, sharing the hope and love we've found in Him with others. As we root ourselves in Jesus, we are equipped and inspired to reflect His love to the world, drawing others into a transformative relationship with Him. Matthew 28:19-20 calls us to this mission: "Therefore go and make disciples of all nations... And surely I am with you always, to the very end of the age."

Sharing our faith is a natural extension of abiding. It flows from an authentic relationship with Christ, driven by gratitude for what He has done in our lives. By sharing our stories, we testify to God's faithfulness and invite others to experience His grace and truth. This evangelistic effort isn't bound by formulas but emerges naturally from the overflow of our relationship with God.

Our personal stories of transformation are powerful tools for introducing others to Christ. They provide relatable, tangible examples of how God works in real lives, making faith approachable and accessible. As we share our experiences, we plant seeds of hope that God can nourish and grow. These stories become beacons of light, demonstrating that change and renewal are possible through Christ.

Colossians 4:5-6 encourages us to "be wise in the way you act toward outsiders; make the most of every opportunity. Let your conversation be always full of grace, seasoned with salt, so that you may know how to answer everyone." This scripture reminds us to approach our mission with wisdom and love, ensuring our interactions reflect Christ's character and compassion.

As we engage in Christ's mission, we are reminded of our role as ambassadors for Him (2 Corinthians 5:20). This identity calls us to reflect His love, truth, and grace in all situations, seeking to understand others and share the Gospel in ways that resonate with their unique stories and backgrounds.

Participating in this mission also enriches our own faith journey. As we see

God at work in the lives of others, our understanding of His power and love deepens. We grow in confidence and joy, witnessing firsthand the impact of sharing our faith.

Today, consider how you can actively participate in Christ's mission. Reflect on your journey with God and identify aspects of your story that reveal His transformative power. Pray for opportunities to share these experiences with others, trusting the Holy Spirit to guide your words and actions.

Embrace this mission with enthusiasm, knowing that as you share the love and hope of Christ, you join a legacy of believers expanding God's kingdom. Through your abiding relationship with Him, become a vessel of His light, inviting others to experience the abundant life found in Jesus. Let your life be a testament to His goodness, inspiring those around you to seek and embrace His love.

Abiding Practice: Share Your Story

Today, step into Christ's mission by sharing your faith experience with a friend or group.

1. **Reflect on Your Faith Journey**: Spend time reflecting on your personal journey with God. Consider key moments of transformation, challenges overcome, and the ways you have experienced God's presence and grace.

2. **Identify Your Story's Core Message**: Determine the central theme or message of your story—perhaps it's about finding hope in a difficult time, experiencing forgiveness, or witnessing God's guidance. Keep it authentic and sincere.

3. **Pray for Guidance and Courage**: Before sharing your story, pray for the Holy Spirit to guide your words and prepare the hearts of those who will hear. Ask for the courage to speak openly and honestly about your experiences.

Example Prayer:
"Lord, open my heart and guide my words as I share my story. Use my experiences to touch others and point them to You. Let Your light shine through my testimony, drawing hearts closer to Your love. Amen."

4. **Choose Your Audience**: Identify a friend, family member, or group where you feel comfortable sharing your story. Seek a setting that allows for meaningful conversation and connection.

5. **Tell Your Story**: Share your faith journey, focusing on how abiding in Christ has transformed your life. Be open to questions and engage in dialogue, allowing others to express their thoughts and reflections.

6. **Invite Interaction**: Encourage your friend or group to share their experiences or any questions they may have about faith. Offer to walk alongside them as they explore their own spiritual journey.

7. **Reflect and Pray**: After sharing, reflect on the experience. Consider the impact on both you and the listener(s). Offer a prayer of gratitude for the opportunity to witness to God's goodness and for the seeds planted through your testimony.

Example Reflection and Prayer:
"Thank You, Lord, for the chance to share my story and testify to Your love. May the words shared resonate with those who heard, drawing them nearer to You. Continue to work in their lives, revealing Your grace and truth. Amen."

By sharing your story, you participate in Christ's mission, embodying His love and inviting others into a life-transforming relationship with Him. Let this practice reinforce the power of testimony and inspire you to continue sharing God's presence, touching hearts and lives with His abundant grace.

WEEK 4: TRANSFORMATIVE ABIDING

Day 24: Abiding in Fruitfulness

Principle: Abiding in Fruitfulness

Fruitfulness is the natural outcome of abiding in Christ. As we remain connected to Him, His life flows through us, producing the fruit of the Spirit that reflects His character and truth. Jesus highlights this in John 15:5: "I am the vine; you are the branches. If you remain in me and I in you, you will bear much fruit; apart from me you can do nothing."

This fruitfulness encompasses qualities such as love, joy, peace, patience, kindness, goodness, faithfulness, gentleness, and self-control, evident in Galatians 5:22-23. These attributes are not self-generated but result from a deep, abiding relationship with Christ, where our lives are transformed by His presence. As the Holy Spirit works within us, these virtues manifest naturally, not as forced behaviors, but as genuine outgrowths of Christ's influence in our lives.

Recognizing and reflecting on the fruit in our lives brings gratitude and encourages us to continue deepening our connection with Christ. By acknowledging these fruits, we see the tangible impact of His work within us and through us, reinforcing our identity in Him. It is a reminder of His faithfulness to cultivate growth in us, even in seasons that seem challenging or dry.

This reflection serves as an opportunity to celebrate God's ongoing transformation in our lives, linking our inner spiritual journey with outward expressions of His grace. As we identify and nurture these qualities, our interactions with others are enriched, revealing God's love and truth in every relationship and circumstance.

The pursuit of a fruitful life is not about striving but about allowing God's Spirit to cultivate growth. As we submit to His leading and remain in His love, we are empowered to pursue His purposes, moving beyond personal ambitions to align with His kingdom work.

Today, take time to reflect on the fruit present in your life. Consider moments where love, patience, or kindness may have impacted those around you. Offer gratitude for God's work and ask Him to continue expanding these qualities in your character.

Seek ways to cultivate these fruits further by engaging in practices that foster deeper connection with Christ—prayer, study, worship, and service. As you abide, let your life reflect the richness of God's Spirit, inspiring others to seek the transformative power of living in Christ.

Through a life marked by spiritual fruitfulness, may you become a beacon of God's love and grace, contributing to the flourishing of His kingdom and drawing others into the abundant life He offers. Let the beauty of your transformed character speak volumes, illuminating the path for those longing to experience the hope and joy found in Christ.

Abiding Practice: Identify Fruits

Today, cultivate awareness of your spiritual growth by reflecting on the fruits evident in your life as a result of abiding in Christ.

1. **Create a Quiet Space**: Choose a peaceful environment where you can focus and reflect without interruptions. Allow yourself to enter a state of mindfulness and receptivity.

2. **Begin with Prayer**: Invite God to guide your reflection and reveal the fruits of His work in your life. Ask for clarity and gratitude for how He is transforming you.

Example Prayer:
"Lord, as I reflect on my journey with You, open my eyes to see the fruits of abiding in Your love. Help me recognize and celebrate Your work in my life, drawing me closer to Your purpose and plans. Amen."

3. **Reflect on Spiritual Growth**: Consider various areas of your life—relationships, attitudes, decisions, and actions. Look for evidence of the fruits of the Spirit developing as a result of your abiding relationship with Jesus.

4. **Identify Specific Fruits**: As you reflect, identify specific fruits that have emerged. How have love, joy, peace, or other qualities grown within you? What changes have you noticed in how you interact with others or face challenges?

5. **Consider the Impact**: Reflect on how the fruitfulness in your life impacts those around you. In what ways has your faith journey inspired or encouraged others? How have your actions reflected Christ's love to the world?

6. **Express Gratitude**: Take time to express gratitude for the fruits identified. Thank God for His transformative power and for equipping you to bear fruit that honors Him.

7. **Commit to Continuous Growth**: Consider how you can continue to cultivate these fruits in your life. Reflect on ways to deepen your abiding relationship and invite ongoing spiritual growth.

Example Reflection and Prayer:
"Thank You, Lord, for the fruits of Your Spirit growing within me. As I celebrate these blessings, guide me to stay connected to You, bearing even more fruit for Your glory. May my life continue to reflect Your love and truth in all I do. Amen."

By identifying the fruits in your life, you affirm the power of abiding in Christ, celebrating the transformation He brings. Let this practice encourage a spirit of gratitude and a commitment to nurturing your connection with Him, allowing His life-giving presence to flourish within you and extend to the world around you.

WEEK 4: TRANSFORMATIVE ABIDING

Day 25: Abiding amid Doubt

Principle: Abiding amid Doubt

Doubt is a natural part of the faith journey, and it's during these moments that abiding in Christ becomes most crucial. Doubt can challenge our beliefs and shake our confidence, yet it also offers an opportunity to deepen our faith and trust in God's promises. When we remain rooted in Christ amid doubt, we invite His truth and presence to steady our hearts and provide assurance.

The Bible is filled with reminders of God's faithfulness, urging us to hold onto His Word even when doubt creeps in. Throughout Hebrews 11, we see many figures who faced uncertainty but continued to abide in faith, trusting in God's plans. These stories show us that doubt does not disqualify us from God's love or service but can lead us to a deeper dependence on Him. James 1:6 encourages us to "believe and not doubt," exhorting us to seek God's wisdom with faith, confident that He hears and responds.

When doubt arises, it's important to bring our concerns to God in prayer, being honest about our fears and uncertainties. Philippians 4:6-7 encourages us to present our requests to God with thanksgiving, promising that His peace will guard our hearts and minds. This practice of transparency with God allows us to release our doubts and receive His reassurance.

By embracing God's promises and affirming His truth over our lives, we cultivate resilient faith that withstands doubt. Abiding amid doubt involves choosing to rely on God's Word as a foundation, letting His voice be louder than our uncertainties. Scriptures like Psalm 119:105, which describes God's Word as a "lamp for my feet, a light on my path," remind us of His guidance and help us navigate through seasons of doubt.

Doubt also invites us into a community of believers where we can find support and encouragement. Sharing our struggles with others allows us to gain perspective and receive prayers that strengthen our faith. Hebrews 10:24-25 encourages us not to give up meeting together but to encourage one another, especially during challenging times.

Today, if doubt is clouding your heart, bring it honestly before God. Reflect on His faithfulness in your life and reaffirm His promises. Engage with Scripture, anchoring yourself in His truth, and consider reaching out to trusted friends or mentors who can walk with you through this season.

Embrace doubt as an opportunity for growth, allowing it to bring you closer to the One who holds all things together. Through your abiding relationship with Christ, may your faith be strengthened, knowing that even amid uncertainty, God's love and truth remain steadfast and unchanging. Let this journey through doubt lead to a deeper, more enduring faith in His unfailing promises.

Abiding Practice: Affirmation

Today, deepen your abiding relationship by writing affirmations based on God's Word to counter doubt and reinforce your faith.

1. **Find a Peaceful Space**: Select a quiet location where you can reflect without distractions. Allow yourself to enter a state of openness and receptivity to God's voice.

2. **Pray for Clarity and Trust**: Begin by asking God for clarity and trust to overcome doubt. Invite the Holy Spirit to guide you as you seek affirmations from Scripture.

Example Prayer:
"Lord, in times of doubt, anchor my heart in Your truth. Open my eyes to see Your promises clearly, and strengthen my faith as I affirm Your Word over my life. Amen."

3. **Search Scripture for Promises**: Spend time reading and meditating on Scripture, looking for specific promises and truths that speak to your current doubts or struggles.

4. **Write Down Affirmations**: Create a list of affirmations based on these scriptures, personalizing them to address your needs and concerns. Let these affirmations remind you of God's character, love, and faithfulness.

Example Affirmations:

- - "I am never alone, for God is with me always. (Matthew 28:20)"
  - "With God's strength, I am capable of overcoming any challenge. (Philippians 4:13)"
  - "God's plans for me are good, granting hope and a future. (Jeremiah 29:11)"
  - "I am loved unconditionally by God, chosen and cherished. (Ephesians 1:4-5)"
5. **Reflect on Each Affirmation**: As you write, reflect on each affirmation, allowing it to settle into your heart and mind. Consider how it speaks to your present concerns and how it might strengthen your trust in God's promises.
6. **Use Regularly for Encouragement**: Keep these affirmations visible—on your mirror, desk, or journal—so that you can revisit them regularly. Use them as tools for encouragement when doubt arises, speaking them aloud in prayer or meditation.
7. **Conclude with Gratitude**: End your time of affirmation by expressing gratitude for God's unchanging character and His Word that guides you through doubt. Commit to abiding in His truth, letting it guide you with confidence and peace.

Example Reflection and Prayer:
"Thank You, Lord, for Your unwavering promises and enduring truth. As I affirm Your Word, strengthen my faith and guide me through doubt with courage and conviction. May Your voice be the foundation upon which I stand. Amen."

By writing and embracing affirmations based on God's Word, you cultivate resilience amid doubt, reinforcing your commitment to abide in His truth and promises. Let this practice draw you closer to God's heart, providing reassurance and confidence as you navigate your faith journey.

WEEK 4: TRANSFORMATIVE ABIDING

Day 26: Abiding in God's Timing

Principle: Abiding in God's Timing

Trusting in God's timing is a vital aspect of our faith journey, inviting us to surrender our timelines and desires to His perfect plan. Abiding in God's timing means being patient and confident, knowing that His wisdom surpasses our understanding and that He orchestrates everything for our good and His glory. Ecclesiastes 3:1 reminds us, "There is a time for everything, and a season for every activity under the heavens."

Waiting on God can be challenging, especially when we long for answers or resolutions. Yet, it's during these seasons of waiting that our faith deepens, as we lean into God's presence and build trust in His divine purposes. These periods of anticipation press us to rely more wholly on Him, transforming our waiting into moments of expectant hope. Abiding in patience allows us to experience His peace and guidance, cultivating resilience and hope even when answers aren't immediate.

Isaiah 40:31 assures us that "those who wait on the Lord shall renew their strength," emphasizing the spiritual renewal that comes from trusting in God's timing. In waiting, we learn to quiet our control and find strength in His promise, acknowledging that His timing often brings outcomes more perfect than our planning.

Patience in prayer is both an act of surrender and a spiritual discipline. By bringing our requests before God while trusting in His timing, we align ourselves with His will, embracing the assurance that He hears us and is actively working on our behalf. Philippians 4:6-7 encourages us to present our requests to God with thanksgiving, allowing His peace to guard our hearts and minds, reinforcing our trust in His timing.

Trusting in God's timing also shifts our focus from immediate gratification to eternal significance. It encourages us to see beyond our current circumstances and understand that waiting cultivates growth and maturity. Romans 5:3-4 speaks of the perseverance and character that emerge from enduring trials, reminding us that waiting is not wasted but purposeful.

During seasons of waiting, we can also find support and encouragement within our faith community. Sharing our journey with others allows us to gather collective wisdom and compassion, hearing stories of how God has acted in His time. Hebrews 10:24-25 encourages communal support, urging us to spur one another on in love and good deeds.

Today, if you find yourself in a season of waiting, invite God into your process. Seek His wisdom and peace, trusting that He orchestrates all things beautifully in His time. Reflect on past moments when God's timing has revealed His purpose, and allow those memories to build your faith.

Embrace the patience of waiting as an opportunity to deepen your relationship with God. Through this trust and surrender, may you find strength and assurance, knowing that His plans are always for your good and His glory. As you align your heart with His timing, experience His peace and presence guiding you every step of the way, leading you into a deeper understanding of His perfect will.

Abiding Practice: Patience in Prayer

Today, practice waiting on God with patience by cultivating a prayer life that embraces His timing.

1. **Create a Calm Environment**: Find a serene space where you can pray and focus without distractions. Settle into a posture of quiet anticipation, inviting God's presence into this moment.

2. **Begin with Surrender**: Start your prayer time by acknowledging God's sovereignty and expressing your desire to align with His timing. Offer your aspirations, concerns, and unanswered prayers to Him with an open heart.

Example Prayer:
"Lord, I recognize that Your timing is perfect, even when I cannot see it. Help me to trust in Your plan for my life and to wait patiently for Your direction and answers. Guide my heart to rest in Your promises. Amen."

3. **Bring Petitions Before God**: Present specific requests or situations where you're seeking God's intervention. Speak or write them down, releasing your expectations and asking for His guidance and clarity.

4. **Embrace the Waiting**: Allow yourself a few moments of silence, sitting in God's presence without expecting immediate answers. Embrace the peace of knowing He is at work, even if outcomes aren't visible.

5. **Reflect on Scripture**: Meditate on Bible verses that remind you of God's faithfulness during waiting seasons. Consider His past actions in your life and Scripture's stories of perseverance and fulfilled promises.

Example Verses:

- "But they who wait for the Lord shall renew their strength." (Isaiah 40:31)
- "Be still before the Lord and wait patiently for Him." (Psalm 37:7)
- "The Lord is good to those who wait for Him, to the soul who seeks Him." (Lamentations 3:25)

6. **Cultivate a Spirit of Patience**: Consider how you can apply patience beyond prayer—living each day with trust and surrender to God's timing. Let this mindset influence your decisions and interactions.

7. **Conclude with Hope**: End your prayer with gratitude for God's work in your life and the assurance of His timing. Resolve to trust and abide in His wisdom, knowing He is faithful to fulfill His promises.

Example Reflection and Prayer:
"Thank You, Lord, for the peace and assurance that come from waiting on Your timing. As I trust in You, fill my heart with hope and patience, guiding me each step of this journey. May I remain steadfast in Your promise, confident that You are working for my good. Amen."

By practicing patience in prayer, you cultivate trust and surrender in God's timing, experiencing His peace and provision amidst uncertainty. Let this practice encourage you to abide in His wisdom, deepening your faith and reliance on His perfect plan for your life.

WEEK 4: TRANSFORMATIVE ABIDING

Day 27: Abiding and Renewal

Principle: Abiding and Renewal

Renewal is an integral part of our spiritual journey, a continuous process of aligning our lives more closely with God's will and purpose. Abiding in Christ invites us into a space where we can experience transformation and revitalization, both spiritually and practically. Romans 12:2 encourages us, "Do not conform to the pattern of this world, but be transformed by the renewing of your mind."

This renewal is more than a change of habit; it's a deepening connection with God that nurtures growth and inspires us to live out our faith with vitality and intention. Through abiding, we invite God to refresh and realign our lives, shedding what hinders us and embracing His life-giving presence. This active participation in renewal allows us to break free from patterns that keep us stagnant, propelling us forward into a life marked by God's grace and purpose.

By choosing to renew specific areas of our lives in dedication to God, we open ourselves to His transformative work, allowing His Spirit to refine us and lead us into greater wholeness and purpose. As we surrender aspects of our lives—our thoughts, attitudes, relationships, and goals—we welcome His guidance and transformation. Ephesians 4:22-24 calls us to "put off your old self" and "put on the new self, created to be like God," highlighting the intentional nature of this renewal process.

This intentional renewal deepens our abiding relationship, fostering spiritual vibrancy and resilience. As we prioritize time in God's Word, prayer, and community, we cultivate a receptive heart that is more attuned to His voice and prompting. The ongoing renewal of our minds and hearts equips us to better discern His will and engage with the world in love and truth.

Renewal is also sustained through practices of spiritual disciplines, such as fasting, solitude, and service, which create space for God to work in and through us. These disciplines reinforce our commitment to transformation, encouraging us to step beyond our comfort zones and stretch our faith.

As we embrace renewal, we gain the strength to persevere through challenges and the wisdom to navigate changing seasons. Colossians 3:10 reminds us to "put on the new self, which is being renewed in knowledge in the image of its Creator," affirming that renewal brings us into deeper alignment with God's image.

Today, reflect on areas of your life that may be longing for renewal. Seek God's guidance in identifying mindsets, habits, or perspectives that need transformation. Invite His Spirit to work within you, reshaping your life according to His will.

Celebrate the ongoing journey of renewal, trusting that God's work in you leads to a flourishing faith. Through this process of renewal, may you find profound peace and purpose, experiencing the joy and freedom that come from living a life intimately connected to God. As you abide in Christ, allow His transformative power to guide you into greater fulfillment and impact.

Abiding Practice: Renew an Area

Today, embrace renewal by choosing an area of your life to dedicate afresh to God.

1. **Reflect on Your Life**: Spend time in quiet reflection, considering different areas of your life—spiritual, emotional, relational, or physical—that may need renewal. Identify an area that the Holy Spirit brings to your attention.

2. **Pray for Guidance and Renewal**: Invite God to guide your thoughts and intentions, seeking His vision for renewal in the chosen area. Ask for clarity and strength to embrace the changes He desires.

Example Prayer:
"Lord, as I seek renewal, open my heart to Your transforming work. Show me the areas that need fresh dedication to You, and grant me the courage to embrace Your plans for my growth and transformation. Amen."

3. **Set Intentions for Renewal**: Determine specific intentions or goals for the area you wish to renew. Outline actionable steps you can

take to dedicate this part of your life to God, whether through new disciplines, attitudes, or practices.

4. **Seek Inspiration from Scripture**: Explore Bible verses that speak to the theme of renewal and transformation. Allow these scriptures to inspire and motivate your journey of renewal.

Example Verses:

- "Create in me a pure heart, O God, and renew a steadfast spirit within me." (Psalm 51:10)
- "Therefore, if anyone is in Christ, the new creation has come: The old has gone, the new is here!" (2 Corinthians 5:17)
- "He refreshes my soul. He guides me along the right paths for his name's sake." (Psalm 23:3)

5. **Implement New Practices**: Begin incorporating the steps and practices that align with your renewal intentions. Approach each action prayerfully, inviting God's presence into every effort and decision.

6. **Reflect on the Journey**: As you progress, regularly reflect on how God is working in this area. Note changes, challenges, and growth, remaining open to His ongoing guidance and refinement.

7. **Commit to Ongoing Renewal**: Dedicate yourself to continuous growth and transformation, seeking to abide in the refreshing presence of God each day. Allow this practice of renewal to reinforce your commitment to living a life rooted in Him.

Example Reflection and Prayer:
"Thank You, Lord, for the renewal You bring to my life. As I commit this area to You, continue to shape and guide me according to Your will. May my life reflect Your glory and transformation, inspiring others to experience Your love and grace. Amen."

By choosing to renew an area of your life, you embrace the transformative power of abiding in Christ, inviting His presence to revitalize and inspire deeper commitment. Let this practice encourage an ongoing journey of growth, reflecting God's work in your life and grounding you more firmly in His love and purpose.

WEEK 4: TRANSFORMATIVE ABIDING

Day 28: Abiding as a Lifestyle

Principle: Abiding as a Lifestyle

Abiding in Christ is not just a momentary practice but a continuous way of living. It involves incorporating rhythms and routines into our lives that consistently draw us closer to God, ensuring that our relationship with Him remains at the center of everything we do. John 15:4 encourages us to "Remain in me, as I also remain in you," inviting us to cultivate a daily walk with Christ that permeates all aspects of our lives.

A Rule of Life is a framework that helps maintain this lifestyle of abiding, integrating spiritual disciplines into our daily routine. Modeled after monastic traditions, such a rule offers structure and intentionality, nurturing our connection with God and guiding our thoughts, actions, and decisions. It serves as a personalized guide to ensure that our daily living reflects our deepest faith commitments and spiritual aspirations.

By consciously setting a Rule of Life, we commit to practices that support our spiritual growth and align our lives with God's purposes. This intentional approach creates space for reflection, worship, service, and rest, enabling us to live with greater peace and clarity. It encourages us to be deliberate in how we prioritize our time and resources, ensuring that our lives are truly centered on our faith.

This framework might include daily practices such as prayer, scripture reading, and meditation, alongside weekly commitments like worship and community service. It's about finding a rhythm that reflects both personal and communal aspects of faith, allowing us to engage with God in multiple dimensions. Philippians 4:9 encourages us to put into practice whatever we have learned and received, ensuring that our actions align with God's teachings and presence.

A Rule of Life is not rigid; it's adaptable to different seasons of life, evolving as we grow spiritually and encounter new challenges and opportunities. Regularly reviewing and adjusting our rule helps us remain responsive to the Spirit's leading while maintaining our commitment to walking closely with Jesus.

In setting this rhythm, we position ourselves to experience God's transformative power daily. By weaving spiritual practices into our lives, we invite Christ's influence into every decision and interaction, fostering a deeper awareness of His presence and a clearer sense of His purpose.

Today, consider creating or revisiting your Rule of Life. Reflect on which practices draw you closer to God and align your heart with His will. Invite the Holy Spirit to guide you in shaping a routine that supports your spiritual journey and empowers you to live faithfully.

As you embrace this intentional living, may you find strength and guidance, growing in your ability to reflect Christ's love in all you do. Through a committed rhythm of abiding, experience the joy and richness of a life anchored in Him, allowing His grace to flow through every aspect of your journey.

Abiding Practice: Write a Rule of Life

Today, establish your personal Rule of Life—an intentional plan for daily drawing close to God and nurturing your abiding relationship.

1. **Reflect on Your Current Rhythms**: Spend time considering your current spiritual practices and daily routines. Identify what draws you closer to God and what might hinder your connection.

2. **Pray for Guidance**: Invite God to guide you as you create your Rule of Life. Ask for insight into the practices that will support your spiritual growth and help you abide more deeply in His presence.

Example Prayer:
"Lord, as I seek to draw closer to You, guide my heart and mind in shaping a Rule of Life that reflects Your love and truth. Help me to establish rhythms that nurture my relationship with You and bring glory to Your name. Amen."

3. **Identify Key Disciplines**: Choose specific spiritual disciplines and practices that foster your connection with God. These might include prayer, scripture reading, worship, service, rest, and community.

4. **Establish Daily, Weekly, Monthly Routines**: Determine a pattern for how you will incorporate these disciplines into your life.

Outline daily practices alongside weekly and monthly commitments, ensuring balance and sustainability.

5. **Write Your Rule of Life**: Document your Rule of Life, detailing the practices you've chosen and the schedule you plan to follow. Be intentional and realistic, allowing room for growth and adaptation as needed.

6. **Reflect and Adjust Regularly**: Commit to reviewing your Rule of Life periodically, reflecting on its effectiveness in drawing you closer to God. Be open to making adjustments to better align your practices with His leading.

7. **Live Out Your Rule**: Begin integrating your Rule of Life into your routine, approaching each day with intention and openness to God's work within and through you.

Example Reflection and Prayer:
"Thank You, Lord, for the opportunity to cultivate a life centered on You. As I live out this Rule of Life, help me to abide more deeply in Your presence and grow in love and grace. May each moment reflect Your glory and draw others to Your light. Amen."

By writing and following a Rule of Life, you embrace a lifestyle of abiding, creating intentional rhythms that anchor you in God's love and guidance. Let this practice enhance your spiritual journey, fostering a daily walk with Christ that transforms and uplifts every aspect of your life.

WEEK 4: TRANSFORMATIVE ABIDING: SMALL GROUP DISCUSSION GUIDE

Ice Breaker:

- "Share a song or quote that has inspired you this week in your walk with God."

Scripture Reading: 2 Corinthians 3:18

- Invite someone to read the verse aloud.
- Discuss how contemplating the Lord's glory and being transformed into His image resonates with your current spiritual journey.

Discussion Questions:

1. **Abiding and Transformation:**
    - How did inviting God to reveal areas for growth impact your awareness of personal transformation?
    - What specific areas did God highlight for you, and how do you plan to embrace change?

2. **Abiding in Mission:**
    - How was your experience sharing your faith story with others? What was the response, and how did it affect you?
    - Why do you think personal stories are powerful tools for sharing God's love and truth?

3. **Abiding in Fruitfulness:**
    - Describe some of the spiritual fruits you identified in your life this week. How do these fruits influence your relationships and decisions?
    - How can you continue to nurture these qualities and encourage their growth in others?

4. **Abiding amid Doubt**:
    - What affirmations based on God's Word did you create to counter doubts, and how did they fortify your faith?
    - How can we support one another in times of doubt and uncertainty?

5. **Abiding in God's Timing**:
    - Can you share a situation where trusting God's timing brought peace or clarity to your life?
    - How does patience in prayer help align your heart with God's plans and timing?

6. **Abiding and Renewal**:
    - What area of your life did you choose to renew, and what steps are you taking in this transformation process?
    - How does intentional renewal impact your overall spiritual journey and connection with God?

7. **Abiding as a Lifestyle**:
    - What key disciplines did you include in your Rule of Life, and how are they helping you maintain a lifestyle of abiding?
    - How can establishing intentional spiritual rhythms enhance our ability to abide in Christ continually?

Application & Action:

- Reflect on a specific aspect of Week 4 that deeply impacted your relationship with Christ. How can you maintain or deepen this practice moving forward?
- How can the group support each member in sustaining their Rule of Life and embracing transformation in their lives?

Prayer:

- Invite participants to share prayer requests related to their experiences with the week's practices and ongoing transformations.

- Close with a group prayer, thanking God for His transformative work and asking for guidance as participants continue to abide more deeply in their walk with Christ.

Closing Thought:

- Encourage group members to remain open to God's work of transformation, trusting His perfect timing and plan. Remind them that abiding in Christ leads to a life of purpose and joy, continually reflecting His love and grace to the world around them.

WEEK 5: LIVING ABIDING EVERY DAY

Day 29: Abiding with Gratitude

Principle: Abiding with Gratitude

Gratitude is an essential component of abiding in Christ, shifting our focus from life's challenges to God's goodness and faithfulness. By cultivating a heart of thankfulness, we recognize His blessings, both big and small, and see His hand at work in our lives. Gratitude enhances our spiritual walk by reinforcing our trust in God's provision and deepening our sense of joy and contentment. 1 Thessalonians 5:16-18 encourages us: "Rejoice always, pray continually, give thanks in all circumstances; for this is God's will for you in Christ Jesus."

Expressing gratitude to God is more than an occasional act; it's a way of life that integrates thankfulness into every aspect of our existence. This posture helps us abide more fully in Christ, fostering a spirit of peace and humility as we acknowledge His presence and gifts. Regular expressions of gratitude remind us of God's constant care and provision, cultivating a heart that worships Him in the midst of both blessings and trials.

One way to deepen this practice is by keeping a gratitude journal, where you regularly note things you are thankful for. This simple act of writing encourages us to look for God's goodness throughout the day, helping us to maintain an attitude of thankfulness. As we reflect on past entries, we see a tapestry of God's faithfulness woven into our lives.

Writing a gratitude letter to God allows us to reflect intentionally on His blessings and express our thanks, reinforcing our awareness of His love and grace in our lives. This practice invites us to pause and consider how God's presence influences our daily experiences, shaping our responses to the world around us.

Incorporating gratitude into our prayer life amplifies our connection to God, turning our focus from what we lack to the abundance of what we already have. By expressing thankfulness as part of our prayers, we align our hearts with His will, acknowledging His hand in all we encounter. Philippians 4:6 emphasizes this, urging us to present our requests to God with thanksgiving, allowing His peace to guard our hearts and minds.

Gratitude also extends beyond personal reflection, influencing our interactions with others. When we recognize the blessing of community, friendships, and family, we become conduits of God's love and grace, expressing appreciation and encouragement. This builds up those around us and strengthens our connections. Colossians 3:15 reminds us to "let the peace of Christ rule in your hearts" and to be thankful, highlighting gratitude's role in fostering unity and harmony.

Today, make gratitude an intentional part of your abiding journey. Begin by taking a moment to thank God for specific blessings in your life, acknowledging His care and provision. Consider how gratitude can transform your perspective and actions, allowing you to experience more fully the joy and peace found in His presence.

As you cultivate a life of thankfulness, may you find yourself more deeply rooted in Christ, experiencing a heightened awareness of His love and a renewed joy in each day. Through this ongoing practice, let gratitude become a cornerstone of your faith, enriching your relationship with God and manifesting His goodness in every facet of your life.

Abiding Practice: Gratitude Letter

Today, deepen your spiritual journey by writing a letter to God expressing your gratitude for His blessings and presence.

1. **Find a Quiet and Reflective Space**: Choose a peaceful location where you can write without distractions. Allow this environment to encourage openness and reflection.

2. **Prepare to Write with Prayer**: Begin with a moment of prayer, inviting the Holy Spirit to guide your thoughts and recollections of God's blessings in your life.

Example Prayer:
"Lord, open my heart to recognize the many ways You have blessed me. Guide my thoughts as I reflect on Your goodness and express my gratitude for all You have done. Amen."

3. **Reflect on God's Blessings**: Take time to ponder the various blessings in your life—relationships, experiences, moments of

grace, answered prayers, and the presence of God in daily living. Consider how these blessings have impacted you.

4. **Write a Letter of Gratitude**: Begin writing your letter to God, expressing your thanks for specific blessings and moments where you have felt His presence. Be sincere and specific, allowing your gratitude to flow honestly and freely.

Example Letter Excerpt:
"Dear God, thank You for the countless ways You have shown Your love and faithfulness. I am grateful for [specific blessing], which has brought joy and peace to my life. Your presence in my daily walk strengthens and uplifts me, and I am truly blessed by Your guiding hand..."

5. **Acknowledge Growth and Learning**: Reflect on how God has helped you grow through challenges and learning experiences. Include these insights in your letter, expressing gratitude for His wisdom and guidance.

6. **Conclude with Praise and Commitment**: End your letter by praising God for His continued work in your life and reaffirming your commitment to live with gratitude and reliance on His grace.

7. **Keep the Letter as a Testament**: Place your gratitude letter in a cherished spot where you can revisit it regularly. Let it serve as a testament to God's love and a reminder to maintain a thankful heart.

Example Reflection and Prayer:
"Thank You, Lord, for Your unwavering love and countless blessings. May my life reflect gratitude for Your goodness each day. Help me to see Your hand in every moment and to cherish Your presence always. Amen."

By writing a gratitude letter to God, you nurture a practice of thankfulness that deepens your abiding relationship with Him, enhancing your awareness of His presence and love. Let this gratitude become a daily expression, infusing your life with joy, peace, and a continual sense of God's goodness.

WEEK 5: LIVING ABIDING EVERY DAY

Day 30: Abiding and Generosity

Principle: Abiding and Generosity

Generosity is a natural outflow of abiding in Christ—it embodies the selfless love and abundant grace we receive from Him. As we remain connected to Jesus, His spirit of giving permeates our hearts, inspiring us to extend kindness and resources to others. In Acts 20:35, we are reminded, "It is more blessed to give than to receive," highlighting the joy and fulfillment found in living generously.

Abiding in Christ nurtures a mindset of abundance rather than scarcity, encouraging us to trust in God's provision and prompting us to give freely without holding back. This perspective transforms how we view our possessions and resources, seeing them not as things to hoard but as blessings to be shared. Generosity reflects God's nature and strengthens our faith as we align our actions with His purposes and engage in His mission to bless the world.

When we practice generosity, we open our hearts to God's leading, allowing Him to use us as conduits of His love and grace. Proverbs 11:25 affirms this principle, stating, "A generous person will prosper; whoever refreshes others will be refreshed." In giving, we experience the refreshing joy and fulfillment that come from investing in the well-being of others.

By choosing to bless others, we participate in God's work and demonstrate His love in tangible ways, creating ripples of compassion and hope that impact lives and communities. Our acts of kindness, whether large or small, become testimonies of God's goodness, pointing others toward His love and care.

Generosity also fosters community and relationships, as it draws people together in shared kindness and mutual support. It cultivates an environment where needs are met, hearts are encouraged, and unity is strengthened. Galatians 6:9-10 encourages us to "do good to all people, especially to those who belong to the family of believers," inviting us to prioritize generosity within our relationships both inside and outside the church.

Living generously does not only involve financial giving; it encompasses our time, talents, and presence as well. Offering a listening ear, volunteering, sharing skills, or simply being present with someone in need are all expressions of generosity that carry the potential for transformative impact.

Today, consider how you can embrace a lifestyle of generosity. Reflect on the resources and gifts you possess, and ask God to reveal opportunities to share them for His glory. Trust that as you give, He will replenish and provide, enriching your life with deeper joy and purpose.

As you cultivate a spirit of generosity, may you become a reflection of Christ's love, inspiring others to experience the fullness of His grace. Through your generous acts, invite the world to witness God's abundant heart, fostering communities of faith and hope that echo His transformative power.

Abiding Practice: Give Freely

Today, embrace the principle of abiding in generosity by choosing a cause or person to bless with a gift.

1. **Reflect on Your Resources**: Consider the resources—time, talents, finances, or possessions—that you have been blessed with. Reflect on how these can be shared with others to make a meaningful impact.

2. **Pray for Direction**: Seek God's guidance in identifying a cause or individual to bless. Ask for discernment and a willingness to give generously and joyfully.

Example Prayer:
"Lord, open my heart to where You are calling me to give freely. Guide me to the person or cause You wish me to bless, and grant me the courage to share Your love and resources abundantly. Amen."

3. **Identify a Cause or Person**: Choose a ministry, non-profit organization, community project, or individual in need. Consider how your gift can support a specific need, foster encouragement, or bring joy.

4. **Decide on the Gift**: Determine what you will give, considering how it can best meet the identified need. It may be a financial donation, volunteering your time, sharing your talents, or providing material assistance.

5. **Give with a Grateful Heart**: As you give, focus on the joy and fulfillment that comes from sharing God's blessings. Approach the act with gratitude and humility, recognizing the privilege of participating in God's work.

6. **Reflect on the Experience**: After giving, take time to reflect on how the act of generosity affected both you and the recipients. Consider the deeper meaning of generosity and how it deepens your abiding relationship with Christ.

7. **Commit to a Generous Lifestyle**: Encourage ongoing generosity by integrating this practice into your daily life. Look for regular opportunities to express generosity, making it a core element of your faith journey.

Example Reflection and Prayer:
"Thank You, Lord, for the opportunity to give freely and share Your love with others. Help me to live with a generous spirit, trusting in Your provision and reflecting Your abundant grace. May my life inspire others to see Your goodness and love. Amen."

By choosing to give freely, you embody the principle of abiding in generosity, participating in God's mission to bless and transform the world. Let this practice of giving enrich your relationship with Christ and inspire you to live a life that reflects His love and compassion to all those you encounter.

WEEK 5: LIVING ABIDING EVERY DAY

Day 31: Abiding and Honesty

Principle: Abiding and Honesty

Honesty is foundational to our relationship with God, inviting us to come before Him with transparency and openness. Abiding in Christ calls us to lay bare our hearts, acknowledging both our strengths and struggles in His presence. Psalm 139:23-24 illustrates this approach: "Search me, God, and know my heart; test me and know my anxious thoughts. See if there is any offensive way in me, and lead me in the way everlasting."

Honest prayer fosters deeper intimacy with God as we allow His truth to penetrate every aspect of our lives. By speaking openly about our struggles, fears, and failures, we invite God to work within us, bringing healing, insight, and transformation. This process of unguarded communication builds trust and aligns us more closely with His will, encouraging a faith that is reflective and genuine.

In moments of honesty and vulnerability, Jesus demonstrated the importance of authentic prayer, seeking connection with the Father during times of trial and temptation. In the Garden of Gethsemane, Jesus laid His heart bare, expressing His anguish and desire, yet ultimately surrendering to God's will (Luke 22:42). This practice of honesty invites us to lay every burden at God's feet, relying on His grace to carry us through, and modeling a relationship rooted in love and trust.

Being honest with God also includes acknowledging our gratitude and joy, sharing our praises alongside our petitions. This holistic approach to prayer fosters a richer dialogue with God, ensuring that every part of our heart is shared with Him. Philippians 4:6 encourages us to present our requests with thanksgiving, framing honesty within the context of gratitude.

True honesty before God requires humility, recognizing that we do not have all the answers and are in continual need of His guidance and wisdom. When we come to God with this posture, we open ourselves to His transformative power, allowing Him to refine our hearts and minds. James 4:8 promises that as we draw near to God, He will draw near to us, offering His presence and support.

Honesty in prayer can lead us to deeper self-awareness, helping us to see our lives more clearly and understand how God is at work within them. Reflecting honestly on our inner life enables us to discern areas that need growth and invites God to lead us forward on the path of righteousness.

Today, approach God with honesty and openness. Take time to examine your heart, sharing both your joys and struggles with Him. Allow this dialogue to strengthen your relationship, making space for God to reveal His presence and purpose in your life.

As you cultivate honesty in your walk with Christ, embrace the freedom and peace that come from being fully known and loved by Him. Let this authenticity spill over into your relationships with others, inviting deeper connections and community rooted in genuine faith and love. Through living honestly before God, find courage and clarity, drawing strength from His unwavering grace.

Abiding Practice: Honest Prayer

Today, deepen your abiding relationship by engaging in honest prayer, speaking openly to God about where you struggle.

1. **Find a Quiet and Safe Space**: Choose a peaceful environment where you can express yourself freely without distraction or interruptions. Allow this space to foster openness and honesty.

2. **Invite God's Presence**: Begin by inviting God to be present with you as you pray. Ask for the courage to speak openly and the grace to receive His truth and guidance.

Example Prayer:
"Lord, as I come before You, help me to lay down my defenses and speak with honesty about my struggles. Open my heart to Your love and wisdom, guiding me through this process of sincerity and revelation. Amen."

3. **Reflect on Your Struggles**: Take time to consider specific areas in your life where you face challenges—whether emotions, behaviors, doubts, or fears. Allow yourself to become aware of any burdens or frustrations weighing heavily on your heart.

4. **Speak Honestly in Prayer**: Share these struggles with God, expressing yourself honestly and without reservation. Trust that He hears you and accepts you as you are, offering compassion and understanding.

Example Honest Prayer:
"Lord, I struggle with [specific issue], and it feels overwhelming. I feel [describe emotions or doubts], and I need Your guidance and strength. Help me overcome these barriers and find peace in Your presence. Amen."

5. **Listen for God's Response**: After sharing your struggles, sit quietly in God's presence, allowing space for His Spirit to speak. Be open to any insights, comfort, or encouragement that arise, trusting in His faithful response.

6. **Reflect on Honest Vulnerability**: Consider how practicing honesty in prayer has impacted your heart and mind. What has God revealed to you, and how might His truth inform your journey going forward?

7. **Commit to Ongoing Openness**: Foster a habit of honest communication with God, inviting Him into every part of your life. Allow this practice to deepen your trust and reliance on His guidance and love.

Example Reflection and Prayer:
"Thank You, Lord, for the gift of honest prayer and the assurance of Your presence. Help me to continue approaching You with openness, trusting in Your love to guide me through my struggles. May my relationship with You be founded on truth and transparency. Amen."

By engaging in honest prayer, you establish a foundation of sincerity and vulnerability with God, nurturing deeper intimacy and trust. Let this practice cultivate a life of abiding in honesty, where you find strength, peace, and transformation through authentic communication with your Creator.

WEEK 5: LIVING ABIDING EVERY DAY

Day 32: Abiding through Listening

Principle: Abiding through Listening

Active listening is a crucial component of abiding deeply with Christ and others. It involves being fully present and attentive, seeking to understand and connect with those around us. James 1:19 advises, "Everyone should be quick to listen, slow to speak and slow to become angry," highlighting the significance of listening in nurturing relationships and maintaining peace.

Listening is an act of love that mirrors our relationship with God, who hears and understands us completely. By practicing active listening, we embody Christ's compassion and attentiveness, creating space for meaningful connection and empathy. This practice fosters deeper relationships with others and enhances our sensitivity to the Holy Spirit's guidance. Just as God listens to our prayers and knows our hearts, we are called to attentively listen to those around us, offering understanding and support.

Active listening requires intentionality and presence, allowing us to engage fully with conversations and demonstrate genuine care. By focusing less on our responses and more on understanding, we honor the person speaking and reflect Christ's love through our interactions. This posture not only strengthens personal relationships but also builds trust and creates an environment where people feel valued and heard.

Practicing active listening involves cultivating a few key habits: giving undivided attention, making eye contact, and providing feedback that indicates understanding, such as nodding or summarizing what the speaker has said. These actions communicate respect and interest, inviting deeper dialogue and connection. Philippians 2:4 encourages us to look not only to our own interests but also to the interests of others, which is a foundational element of true listening.

In addition to human interactions, active listening enhances our spiritual walk by heightening our awareness of God's voice. Through prayer and meditation on Scripture, we can attune our hearts to the Holy Spirit, discerning His guidance in our lives. John 10:27 tells us, "My sheep listen to my voice; I know them, and they follow me." By cultivating a listening spirit, we align ourselves more closely with God's will and deepen our abiding relationship with Him.

Today, practice active listening in your conversations and spiritual life. Set aside distractions and make a conscious effort to be present with those you encounter, whether in person or through digital interactions. Extend this listening posture to your time with God, inviting Him to speak into your heart and mind.

As you refine this skill, you will find that active listening enriches your connections and expands your understanding, allowing you to more fully embody Christ's love and compassion. Through genuine listening, may you become a channel of peace and empathy, drawing others closer to God and reflecting His attentive care in every interaction.

Abiding Practice: Active Listening

Today, practice abiding through listening by engaging in a conversation with active listening as a focus.

1. **Choose a Conversation**: Identify a conversation with a friend, family member, colleague, or even a new acquaintance where you can practice active listening. Prioritize a setting that encourages uninterrupted dialogue.

2. **Prepare with Prayer**: Before engaging in the conversation, pray for openness and attentiveness. Ask God to help you listen with empathy and understanding, placing His love at the center of your interaction.

Example Prayer:
"Lord, help me to listen wholeheartedly and engage genuinely in this conversation. Grant me the patience and presence to hear and understand, reflecting Your love in all I do. Amen."

3. **Be Present and Focused**: Enter the conversation with the intention of being fully present. Set aside distractions, whether physical (like your phone) or mental, and commit to focusing entirely on the speaker.

4. **Use Active Listening Techniques**: As you listen, apply active listening techniques, such as maintaining eye contact, nodding or giving verbal affirmations, refraining from interrupting, and reflecting back what you hear to ensure understanding.

5. **Seek to Understand**: Make a conscious effort to delve deeper into the speaker's thoughts and feelings. Ask open-ended questions if appropriate, and express genuine curiosity and care for their perspective.

6. **Reflect on the Experience**: After the conversation, spend time reflecting on the practice of active listening. Consider how it influenced the interaction and any insights or connections formed as a result.

7. **Commit to Ongoing Listening**: Resolve to incorporate active listening into your daily interactions, fostering deeper connections and empathy. Allow this practice to nurture relationships and offer moments of presence, reflecting Christ's attentive love.

Example Reflection and Prayer:
"Thank You, Lord, for the opportunity to practice active listening and connect deeply with others. Help me to continue aligning my heart with Christ's example of love and attentiveness, seeking to fully understand and care for those around me. Amen."

By practicing active listening, you embody the principle of abiding through presence and understanding, creating a space where relationships can flourish. Let this practice deepen your connections and align your interactions with Christ's love, enriching both your spiritual journey and the lives of those you touch.

WEEK 5: LIVING ABIDING EVERY DAY

Day 33: Abiding in God's Strength

Principle: Abiding in God's Strength

Abiding in Christ empowers us to draw strength from His presence, enabling us to face challenges with courage and conviction. When we rest in God's strength, we find the courage to step beyond our comfort zones and trust Him to lead us into new territories. Philippians 4:13 reassures us, "I can do all this through him who gives me strength," emphasizing our reliance on God's power rather than our limited abilities.

Abiding in God's strength involves aligning our lives with His purposes, trusting that He will equip and sustain us for the journey ahead. This reliance requires us to leap forward in faith, believing that God is faithful and trustworthy. As we embrace His strength, we acknowledge that our own abilities are insufficient, and we open ourselves to the boundless possibilities that come from His divine support.

Exercising faith invites us to embrace opportunities for growth and transformation, guided by God's wisdom and prompting. By taking steps of faith, we participate in His mission, witnessing His power as we allow Him to work through us, even in our vulnerability. This journey of faith is not absent of challenges, but with each step, we become more attuned to His leading and confident in His provision.

Stepping out in faith requires us to relinquish control and embrace the unknown, trusting that God's path will lead to greater understanding and fulfillment. Hebrews 11:1 defines faith as "confidence in what we hope for and assurance about what we do not see," affirming the unseen potential found within God's promises and power.

In moments of uncertainty or fear, we can turn to God in prayer, asking Him to strengthen and guide us. Isaiah 41:10 encourages us, "Do not fear, for I am with you; do not be dismayed, for I am your God. I will strengthen you and help you; I will uphold you with my righteous right hand." This assurance allows us to navigate life's challenges with a foundation of trust and faithfulness.

As we step out in faith, God often expands our hearts and perspectives, revealing new depths of His love and faithfulness. We grow in resilience and adaptability, discovering that His strength is made perfect in our weakness, as Paul experienced in 2 Corinthians 12:9: "My grace is sufficient for you, for my power is made perfect in weakness."

Today, consider areas where you might be called to exercise faith and rely on God's strength. Whether it's pursuing a new opportunity, engaging in ministry, or facing a personal challenge, invite God to lead and empower you.

As you abide in His strength, may you experience the courage and joy that comes from trusting in His plans. Let His presence guide you confidently into the future, assured that He is with you every step of the way. Through your reliance on His strength, become a living testament to His faithfulness and love, inspiring others to seek and trust in His transforming power.

Abiding Practice: Exercise Faith

Today, step into God's call by exercising faith in an area where He is leading you, trusting in His strength to sustain and guide you.

1. **Identify an Area of Leading**: Reflect on areas or opportunities where you sense God prompting you to step out in faith. This may be a project at work, a relationship that needs healing, sharing your faith, or a personal growth opportunity.

2. **Pray for Courage and Guidance**: Seek God's direction and strength as you prepare to exercise faith in this specific area. Invite the Holy Spirit to fill you with courage and confidence to move forward.

Example Prayer:
"Lord, I trust in Your strength and guidance as I step out in faith. Help me to align with Your will, assured of Your presence and power. Grant me the courage to follow Your leading faithfully. Amen."

3. **Take a Step of Faith**: Consciously take a practical step toward the area God is leading you. Let your actions be fueled by trust in God's promises, even if uncertainty or fear is present.

4. **Rely on God's Strength**: As you move forward, lean on God's strength, remembering that He equips you for all He asks. Let go of control and trust in His provision and direction.

5. **Reflect on the Experience**: After taking the step, reflect on the experience. Consider how God's strength manifested in the moment and what you learned through the act of faith.

6. **Celebrate God's Faithfulness**: Express gratitude for God's presence and power in this journey. Celebrate the growth and insights gained, acknowledging His work in your life.

7. **Commit to Continual Faith Steps**: Resolve to make exercising faith an ongoing practice, remaining open to God's direction and strength in all areas of your life.

Example Reflection and Prayer:
"Thank You, Lord, for Your steadfast strength and guidance as I journey in faith. May I continue to trust and rely on You, taking steps that honor Your name and reflect Your power. Let my life be a testament to Your faithfulness and greatness. Amen."

By exercising faith and relying on God's strength, you embrace the principle of abiding in His power, inviting transformation and growth in your life as you walk courageously in His leading. Let this practice deepen your trust and demonstrate His love and strength through every step of faith you take.

WEEK 5: LIVING ABIDING EVERY DAY

Day 34: Abiding and Trust

Principle: Abiding and Trust

Abiding in Christ includes deepening our trust in His faithful guidance. Trusting God requires letting go of control, believing in His promises, and remaining confident in His plans, especially when the path ahead is unclear. Proverbs 3:5-6 encourages us: "Trust in the Lord with all your heart and lean not on your own understanding; in all your ways submit to him, and he will make your paths straight."

Trust is foundational to our relationship with God. It involves recognizing His sovereignty and learning to rest in His care. Through trust, we can navigate life's uncertainties with peace, assured of His presence and direction. By trusting in Him rather than our own understanding, we allow God's wisdom to illuminate our path, making the journey secure, even when it feels unpredictable.

Abiding and trust lead us to a deeper relationship with God, where His love and wisdom guide our every step. This relationship fosters a sense of security and confidence, knowing that God is intimately aware of our needs and walks beside us in all circumstances. Jeremiah 29:11 reminds us of God's good intentions for us: "For I know the plans I have for you," declares the Lord, "plans to prosper you and not to harm you, plans to give you hope and a future."

A trust walk offers us an opportunity to reflect on God's leading, reminding us of His faithfulness and renewing our confidence in His steadfast presence. As we walk with God, both literally and metaphorically, we can reflect on His past faithfulness, how He has guided us through difficult times, and the ways in which He continues to work in our lives. It is an invitation to listen for His voice, discern His guidance, and strengthen our resolve to follow Him wholeheartedly.

This exercise in trust can involve daily practices like journaling about God's past provisions, spending time in prayer and meditation on His Word, and sharing testimonies of His faithfulness with others. Each act of remembering and reflecting on God's work reinforces our trust and provides encouragement for the challenges we face.

Letting go of control and entrusting our lives to God requires a purposeful decision to rely on His strength and direction. Courageously stepping out in faith, even when we are uncertain, invites His transformative power to refine us and align us more closely with His will. Isaiah 26:3 reminds us, "You will keep in perfect peace those whose minds are steadfast, because they trust in you."

Today, embrace opportunities to trust God more fully. Consider areas of your life where you need to surrender control, inviting Him to guide your steps and shape your decisions. Pray for strength to trust in His timing and wisdom, even when the way ahead seems unclear.

As you deepen your trust in God's guidance, experience the peace and assurance that come from abiding in His presence. Let this trust be a beacon of hope and inspiration, inspiring others to place their confidence in God's unfailing promises and love. Through trust, may your life reflect a steadfast faith, anchored in the One who leads us faithfully.

Abiding Practice: Trust Walk

Today, engage in a trust walk, reflecting on God's guidance and faithfulness as you journey with Him.

1. **Choose Your Path**: Select a familiar route for your walk, a place where you can reflect and be alone with your thoughts. Consider a local park, a quiet neighborhood, or a trail where you can connect with God's creation.

2. **Begin with Prayer**: As you start your walk, invite God to join you, asking for a heightened awareness of His presence and a heart open to trusting His guidance.

Example Prayer:
"Lord, as I walk today, help me reflect on Your faithful guidance and renew my trust in Your plans for me. Show me how You have led me safely thus far, and strengthen my faith in Your continued presence. Amen."

3. **Reflect on God's Leading**: As you walk, reflect on the ways God has guided and protected you throughout your life. Consider

specific instances, both recent and past, where His hand was evident in directing your path.

4. **Acknowledge God's Faithfulness**: Take note of the moments when God's provision, wisdom, or protection was particularly clear. Acknowledge how His faithfulness has brought you through challenges and forward in growth.

5. **List Lessons Learned**: As you consider your journey, recognize the lessons learned and insights gained through God's leading. What have these experiences taught you about God's character and love?

6. **Embrace Trust for the Future**: Turn your thoughts toward the present and future, inviting God to continue leading you. Consider areas where you desire His guidance and express your readiness to follow His direction with trust.

7. **Conclude with Gratitude**: As your walk concludes, offer a prayer of gratitude for God's faithfulness and unwavering care. Commit to trusting Him wholeheartedly with all paths ahead.

Example Reflection and Prayer:
"Thank You, Lord, for the countless ways You have led and sustained me. As I continue this journey, let my trust in Your guidance deepen, knowing You walk beside me with love and wisdom. May my life reflect the confidence I find in You. Amen."

By taking a trust walk, you reaffirm your abiding trust in God's faithful guidance, reflecting on His past care and reinforcing your confidence in His future provision. Let this practice strengthen your relationship with Christ, equipping you to journey forward with peace and trust in His unfailing love.

WEEK 5: LIVING ABIDING EVERY DAY

Day 35: Abiding and Reconciliation

Principle: Abiding and Reconciliation

Abiding in Christ empowers us to foster reconciliation, restoring peace and unity in our relationships. As followers of Christ, we are called to be agents of healing and restoration, mirroring His reconciling love and grace. Jesus taught the importance of reconciliation in Matthew 5:23-24, where He encourages us to seek peace with others before offering gifts at the altar. This emphasizes the high value God places on harmonious relationships within the body of believers and beyond.

Reconciliation is not only about resolving conflict but also about restoring relationships to wholeness and harmony. It involves humility, forgiveness, and a willingness to let God's love transcend our hurt and differences. Through humility, we acknowledge our need for God's grace and the grace of others, paving the way for healing and understanding. When we abide in Christ, we draw strength and wisdom from Him, enabling us to extend grace and seek reconciliation with others.

Reconciliation requires us to take the initiative, reaching out to those we've hurt or who have hurt us, offering genuine apologies and seeking forgiveness. This process can be challenging, but it is transformative and rich with opportunities for growth. Colossians 3:13 reminds us, "Bear with each other and forgive one another if any of you has a grievance against someone. Forgive as the Lord forgave you." This underscores our call to forgive freely, modeling the abundant forgiveness we have received in Christ.

By reaching out to mend broken relationships, we participate in God's reconciling work, allowing His peace and love to flourish in our lives and communities. This participation reflects the essence of Christ's mission, which is to reconcile all creation to Himself. As Paul writes in 2 Corinthians 5:18-19, God "gave us the ministry of reconciliation" and entrusted us with the message of reconciliation, calling us to reflect this on earth as it is in heaven.

Actively pursuing reconciliation fosters an environment of trust and unity, breaking down barriers and building bridges. It cultivates communities where grace and truth reign, encouraging mutual respect and understanding. Through this commitment, we demonstrate the power of abiding in Christ, transforming not only our hearts but also the world around us.

Today, reflect on any relationships in need of reconciliation and seek God's guidance in taking steps towards healing. Pray for the courage to initiate these conversations and the grace to listen and forgive. Invite the Holy Spirit to guide and empower your interactions, that they may reflect Christ's love.

As you engage in the work of reconciliation, may you experience the fullness of God's peace, knowing that your efforts are part of a greater kingdom purpose. Let this journey of healing inspire and encourage others, drawing them into a deeper understanding of God's redemptive love. Through abiding in Christ, become a beacon of reconciliation, bringing wholeness and unity to your relationships and community.

Abiding Practice: Seek Reconciliation

Today, embrace the principle of abiding through reconciliation by reaching out to mend a strained or broken relationship.

1. **Identify a Relationship in Need**: Reflect on your relationships and identify someone with whom you need to seek reconciliation. Consider the nature of the misunderstanding or rift and your desire to bring healing.

2. **Pray for Guidance and Humility**: Seek God's guidance, strength, and humility as you embark on this journey. Ask for wisdom, grace, and an open heart as you extend the olive branch.

Example Prayer:
"Lord, grant me the humility and courage to seek reconciliation in this relationship. Fill me with Your love and wisdom as I reach out with sincerity and strive to restore peace and understanding. Amen."

3. **Reach Out with Intention**: Initiate contact with the person you've identified. Approach them with honest intentions, expressing your desire to reconcile and restore the relationship.

4. **Communicate with Compassion**: When discussing the issue, prioritize active listening and empathy. Share your perspectives gently, acknowledge any mistakes, and be open to hearing their point of view.

5. **Offer and Seek Forgiveness**: Be prepared to offer forgiveness for past hurts and to seek forgiveness for any wrongs. Allow God's love to guide you in this process of healing and restoration.

6. **Commit to Growth and Understanding**: Reflect on the situation and identify ways to prevent future misunderstandings. Commit to nurturing compassion, understanding, and trust within the relationship.

7. **Thank God for His Reconciling Work**: Conclude with gratitude for the opportunity to participate in God's reconciling work. Thank Him for His love and for guiding you toward peacemaking in your relationships.

Example Reflection and Prayer:
"Thank You, Lord, for Your grace and love that make reconciliation possible. As I seek to restore this relationship, may Your peace and wisdom guide me. Help me to grow in understanding and compassion, honoring You in all my interactions. Amen."

By seeking reconciliation, you embody the principle of abiding through love and peacemaking, fostering healing and unity in your relationships. Let this practice be a testament to God's reconciling power, allowing His love to transform and nurture every corner of your life and community.

WEEK 5: LIVING ABIDING EVERY DAY: SMALL GROUP DISCUSSION GUIDE

Ice Breaker:

- Share a moment from this past week where you felt particularly connected to someone or something—be it a conversation, place, or activity—and what made it special or significant for you.

Discussion Outline:

Day 29: Abiding with Gratitude

- **Principle Discussion:** Discuss the role of gratitude in deepening our relationship with Christ. How does gratitude shift our perspective from challenges to blessings?

- **Practice Reflection:** Share the experience of writing a gratitude letter to God. How did this practice enhance your awareness of His presence and blessings in your life?

- **Application:** How can you incorporate gratitude into your daily life? What changes might you expect to see?

Day 30: Abiding and Generosity

- **Principle Discussion:** Explore how abiding in Christ naturally leads to generous living. Why is generosity a crucial aspect of our faith walk?

- **Practice Reflection:** Discuss the act of giving freely. What insights or emotions emerged when you chose someone or something to bless? How did it feel to trust in God's provision while giving?

- **Application:** How can you cultivate a lifestyle of generosity beyond financial gifts? Share ways to consistently express generosity in your community.

Day 31: Abiding and Honesty

- **Principle Discussion:** Talk about the importance of honesty in prayer and how it fosters deeper intimacy with God. How does presenting our true selves in prayer transform our relationship with Him?

- **Practice Reflection:** Reflect on the honest prayer practice. How did it feel to lay your struggles before God? Did you receive any new insights or comfort?
- **Application:** Commit to open communication with God. How can honesty in prayer help in other relationships in your life?

Day 32: Abiding through Listening

- **Principle Discussion:** Consider the value of active listening in cultivating relationships. How does listening reflect Christ's attentiveness and love?
- **Practice Reflection:** Share experiences of practicing active listening. How did this change the dynamics of the conversation? What was challenging about this practice?
- **Application:** How can active listening enhance your relationships at home or work? Discuss ways to become a better listener.

Day 33: Abiding in God's Strength

- **Principle Discussion:** Discuss the concept of drawing strength from God when stepping out in faith. What are the blessings of relying on His strength over our own?
- **Practice Reflection:** Share experiences from the day's "Exercise Faith" activity. What did you do, and how did God's strength manifest for you?
- **Application:** Talk about areas in life where you feel called to exercise faith. How can you encourage each other to take these steps?

Day 34: Abiding and Trust

- **Principle Discussion:** Explore what it means to trust God wholeheartedly. How does trusting God change your approach to life's uncertainties?

- **Practice Reflection:** Reflect on the trust walk. How did contemplating God's past guidance reinforce your faith in His plans for the future?

- **Application:** Identify areas where trust needs to deepen and share strategies to strengthen your reliance on God.

Day 35: Abiding and Reconciliation

- **Principle Discussion:** Converse about the role of reconciliation in living out Christ's love. Why is it vital for fostering peace and unity?

- **Practice Reflection:** Share your experiences of seeking reconciliation. What fears or hesitations did you face, and how did engaging in this act of peacemaking impact you?

- **Application:** Discuss how this practice can transform relationships and lead to personal growth. How can the principles of forgiveness and reconciliation be integrated into everyday life?

Closing Prayer: Conclude with a group prayer, thanking God for His presence throughout your discussions and asking for His guidance in applying these principles in your daily lives. Invite each participant to share a brief prayer request related to the topics discussed that day.

WEEK 6: CONTINUAL ABIDING

Day 36: Abiding through Forgiveness

Principle: Abiding through Forgiveness

Forgiveness is a cornerstone of abiding in Christ, reflecting His grace and mercy in our lives. Through forgiving others, we release the burden of past hurts and open our hearts to healing and renewal. In Ephesians 4:32, we are reminded, "Be kind and compassionate to one another, forgiving each other, just as in Christ God forgave you." This scripture highlights that our capacity to forgive is rooted in the forgiveness we have already received through Christ.

Forgiving others mirrors the forgiveness we have received from God, allowing His love to free us from resentment and bitterness. It is an act of obedience and liberation, inviting peace into our hearts and relationships. By choosing to forgive, we break the chains that bind us to past grievances, fostering reconciliation and a fresh start for both ourselves and those we forgive.

Forgiveness is not about condoning wrong actions, but about choosing to release the hold those actions have on our hearts. It is an intentional decision to let go of anger and pain, making room for God's healing to enter our lives. Through this act, we practice compassion and align ourselves more closely with God's heart and purpose.

The practice of writing down past hurts and actively choosing to forgive is a powerful step toward healing and peace. By articulating these grievances and then releasing them in prayer, we can physically and spiritually hand over our burdens to God. This act of surrender empowers us to abide more fully in God's presence and love, as we trust Him to mend what is broken.

Forgiveness cultivates a heart of empathy, encouraging us to see others through God's eyes and respond with kindness. It strengthens our faith and enhances our capacity to love unconditionally, as we experience the transformative power of divine mercy working within us.

Through forgiveness, we not only find personal peace but also contribute to a more compassionate and unified community. As we forgive, we create an atmosphere where grace abounds, encouraging a cycle of forgiveness that can ripple out into greater healing.

Today, reflect on any lingering hurts and consider taking steps toward forgiveness. Begin by listing those offenses, praying over them, and asking God for the strength and grace to forgive as you have been forgiven. Invite the Holy Spirit to fill your heart with peace and guide you on this journey toward liberation.

As you embrace forgiveness, may you discover new depths of freedom and joy, unencumbered by the weight of past wounds. Through this practice, nurture a heart that abides in Christ, living out His love and compassion in your relationships and community. Let forgiveness become a testament to His transforming grace, drawing others to seek and experience God's boundless mercy.

Abiding Practice: Forgive Others

Today, deepen your abiding relationship with Christ by forgiving others, writing down past hurts, and embracing healing.

1. **Create a Safe and Reflective Space**: Find a quiet location where you can reflect and pray without interruptions. Allow this space to encourage openness and vulnerability.

2. **Pray for Guidance and Strength**: Invite God to guide you through the process of forgiveness. Ask for the strength to release past hurts and the courage to forgive, letting His love empower you.

Example Prayer:
"Lord, I come before You with a willing heart to forgive. Guide me through this process, granting me the strength to let go of past hurts and embrace Your healing love. Amen."

3. **Reflect on Past Hurts**: Spend time reflecting on relationships or situations where you have experienced hurt or pain. Allow yourself to become aware of the emotions and memories associated with these experiences.

4. **Write Down Specific Hurts**: As you reflect, write down the specific hurts or offenses you wish to forgive. Describe how these

experiences have impacted you, acknowledging your emotions without judgment.

5. **Actively Choose to Forgive**: Consciously choose to forgive each person or situation you have listed. Speak or write words of forgiveness, allowing your heart to release the burden and bitterness associated with these hurts.

Example Forgiveness Statement:
"I forgive [Name/Offense], releasing them and the pain they have caused me. I choose to let go of bitterness and embrace God's healing and peace in my life. Amen."

6. **Invite God's Healing and Peace**: After forgiving, spend time in prayer, inviting God's healing and peace to fill your heart. Envision His love enveloping you, bringing renewal and comfort.

7. **Commit to Living in Forgiveness**: Dedicate yourself to living a life characterized by forgiveness and grace. Allow this practice to inspire ongoing compassion, understanding, and reconciliation in all your relationships.

Example Reflection and Prayer:
"Thank You, Lord, for the freedom and healing found in forgiveness. As I embrace Your grace, help me to live a life of love and compassion, reflecting Your mercy to others. May my heart remain open to Your continual work of healing and renewal. Amen."

By practicing forgiveness, you embody the principle of abiding through grace and compassion, inviting God's healing into your heart and relationships. Let this practice deepen your connection with Christ, fostering peace and renewal in every area of your life.

WEEK 6: CONTINUAL ABIDING

Day 37: Abiding in Rest Revisited

Principle: Abiding in Rest

Rest is a vital aspect of abiding in Christ, inviting us to cease from our labor and be refreshed in His presence. In the midst of life's demands, resting in God allows us to find peace, renewal, and clarity as we reconnect with the source of our strength and hope. Matthew 11:28 provides the comforting invitation from Jesus: "Come to me, all you who are weary and burdened, and I will give you rest." This call from Christ reminds us that true rest is found not in the absence of activity, but in His loving embrace.

Abiding in rest fosters a deeper awareness of God's love and provision. As we intentionally pause from our work and worries, we draw into a place of stillness where we can listen to His voice, aligning our hearts with His will. Rest is not merely physical; it is a holistic re-centering of our mind, body, and spirit in the divine presence. Psalm 46:10 encourages us to "Be still, and know that I am God," inviting us to experience His sovereignty and peace.

This practice of rest refreshes our souls, providing the space needed to reflect on God's goodness and gain perspective on our lives. It allows us to release the burdens we carry, trusting in God's timing and care, and to restore our energy and focus. Through rest, we are reminded of our dependence on Him, fostering humility and gratitude.

Practicing rest in silence offers a serene opportunity to disengage from the noise and busyness of life, allowing God's peace to renew and restore us. This intentional quiet can be a time of prayerful reflection, meditative reading of Scripture, or simply sitting with God in silent communion. Such practices help cultivate an awareness of His presence, grounded in His peace.

Integrating regular times of rest into our rhythm of life not only benefits our personal well-being but also enriches our relationships and service. When we are rested, we can engage with others more fully, embodying Christ's love and grace with a renewed spirit. Isaiah 40:31 reminds us of the strength found in God: "But those who hope in the Lord will renew their strength. They will soar on wings like eagles."

Today, consider ways to incorporate rest into your daily or weekly routine. Make it a priority to set aside moments for stillness and reflection, intentionally pulling away from the pressures of daily life. Allow God's peace to permeate your heart and mind, renewing you from within.

As you embrace the practice of rest, may you encounter the richness of God's presence, discovering deeper peace and clarity. Through this rhythm of abiding rest, let your life be a reflection of His strength and love, refreshed to serve and love others. Trust that in your resting, God is at work, equipping you for the journey He has set before you.

Abiding Practice: Rest in Silence

Today, deepen your abiding relationship by spending ten minutes in silence with God, resting in His peaceful presence.

1. **Create a Calming Environment**: Find a quiet space where you can be comfortable and free from distractions. Consider elements such as soft lighting or a comfortable seat that help create a restful atmosphere.

2. **Invite God's Presence**: Begin by inviting God's presence into this moment of silence. Acknowledge your desire to rest in Him and receive His peace.

Example Prayer:
"Lord, I come to You seeking rest and renewal. Quiet my mind and heart as I enter Your presence, and fill this time of silence with Your peace and love. Amen."

3. **Set a Timer for Ten Minutes**: Use a timer to mark the ten minutes of silence, allowing you to focus fully on resting in God without checking the clock.

4. **Embrace the Stillness**: As the silence begins, let go of any thoughts or concerns. Allow your mind to settle into the quiet, inviting God's peace to envelop you like a warm embrace.

5. **Focus on Being Present**: Concentrate on being fully present with God in this moment. As thoughts come and go, gently redirect

your focus to resting in His love. You might use gentle breathing or a simple phrase like "God is with me" to maintain focus.

6. **Listen for God's Whisper**: Be open to anything God might impress upon your heart during this time, whether through a sense of peace, comfort, or a specific thought or impression.

7. **Reflect and Give Thanks**: As the timer ends, slowly bring your time of silence to a close. Reflect on the experience and express gratitude for God's presence and the rest you've received.

Example Reflection and Prayer:
"Thank You, Lord, for this time of rest in Your presence. As I return to the demands of my day, let the peace I've found here continue to renew and sustain me. May I always remember the refuge I have in You. Amen."

By practicing rest in silence, you cultivate a habit of abiding in God's peace, allowing His presence to refresh and restore you. Let this practice become a daily rhythm that enhances your spiritual journey, infusing your life with tranquility and a deepened awareness of God's love.

WEEK 6: CONTINUAL ABIDING

Day 38: Abiding and Vision

Principle: Abiding and Vision

Abiding in Christ invites us to align our lives with His broader vision, embracing the dreams and purposes He has set before us. Recognizing and pursuing God's vision allows us to live with intention and clarity, guided by His wisdom and grace. Proverbs 29:18 reminds us, "Where there is no vision, the people perish," highlighting the importance of discerning and following God's path for our lives.

Vision in the context of abiding is not just about setting goals; it's about seeking God's heart for our lives and letting His desires shape our dreams and ambitions. It involves prayerfully considering how our unique gifts and opportunities can align with His kingdom purposes, allowing His dreams for us to become our own. This alignment requires a heart tuned to His voice, ready to embrace His plans over our own desires.

By dreaming with God, we open ourselves to the possibilities He envisions, nurturing a sense of purpose and direction as we follow His leading. Our dreams become reflections of His greater story, and our lives, canvases where His will is painted through us. This vision gives us hope and clarity, empowering us to take steps that are consistent with His intentions.

Engaging with God's vision compels us to regularly seek His guidance in prayer and reflection, asking Him to reveal His plans and insights. Jeremiah 29:11 provides assurance of His good intentions, stating, "For I know the plans I have for you," declares the Lord, "plans to prosper you and not to harm you, plans to give you hope and a future."

Embracing God's vision often involves embracing change, as He may lead us into new territories or push us beyond our comfort zones. This journey requires courage and faith, trusting that His plans are for our ultimate good and His glory. Philippians 2:13 reassures us that "it is God who works in you to will and to act in order to fulfill his good purpose," affirming His active role in bringing our God-inspired dreams to fruition.

Today, consider what God's vision for your life might include. Spend time in prayer, asking Him to reveal His desires and purposes for you. Reflect on how your talents and experiences can play a role in His kingdom work and seek His wisdom to discern your next steps.

As you embrace God's vision, may you experience a renewed sense of purpose and direction, feeling aligned with His heart and equipped for the journey ahead. Through this alignment, let your life bear witness to the beauty and power of living a life led by His vision, inspiring others to seek and follow God's path for themselves. Let your dreams become a collaboration with the Divine, partnering with Him to bring His kingdom more fully to earth.

Abiding Practice: Dream with God

Today, engage with God's vision for your life by spending time in prayer, inviting Him to reveal His dreams and purposes for you.

1. **Prepare a Quiet Space**: Find a serene place where you can focus and dream without interruptions. Use elements that inspire reflection, like soft music or a view of nature, to facilitate openness to God's voice.

2. **Begin with a Heart of Openness**: Start your time with a prayer of openness, expressing your desire to align with God's vision for your life. Acknowledge His sovereignty and wisdom in guiding your journey.

Example Prayer:
"Lord, as I spend time in Your presence, open my heart to Your vision and dreams for my life. Help me to see beyond my limitations and discern Your purposes with clarity and faith. Amen."

3. **Reflect on Your Gifts and Passions**: Consider the unique talents, passions, and experiences God has given you. Reflect on how these might align with His vision for your life and the impact you feel called to make.

4. **Seek God's Vision through Prayer**: Enter into a time of prayer, asking God to reveal His dreams for your life. Invite the Holy Spirit to speak to your heart, guiding you toward His desires and plans.

5. **Listen for God's Voice**: As you pray, remain open and attentive to any impressions, thoughts, or scriptures that surface. Trust that God's Spirit is at work, revealing glimpses of His vision.

6. **Record Your Reflections**: Write down any insights, ideas, or prompts that arise during your time of prayer. Consider how these might shape your goals and decisions moving forward, seeking confirmation through God's Word and counsel.

7. **Commit to God's Vision**: Offer a prayer of commitment, expressing your willingness to pursue God's vision for your life with trust and courage. Ask for continued guidance as you take steps toward living out His purposes.

Example Reflection and Prayer:
"Thank You, Lord, for revealing Your vision for my life. As I embrace Your dreams as my own, grant me the faith and courage to follow where You lead. May my journey reflect Your glory and bring Your kingdom closer. Amen."

By dreaming with God, you draw closer to His heart and deepen your abiding relationship, aligning your life with His beautiful vision for you. Let this practice inspire a journey of purpose and fulfillment as you walk boldly in His plans, trusting in His wisdom and love to guide every step.

WEEK 6: CONTINUAL ABIDING

Day 39: Continuously Abiding

Principle: Continuously Abiding

Continuously abiding in Christ involves a seamless integration of our faith into every moment and aspect of life. It means living with an awareness of His presence and allowing His influence to permeate our thoughts, actions, and interactions. John 15:7 captures this beautifully, "If you remain in me and my words remain in you, ask whatever you wish, and it will be done for you." This ongoing connection is key to experiencing the fullness of life that God intends, characterized by peace, purpose, and abundance.

To abide in Christ continuously, we cultivate practices that foster this unwavering connection. Regular prayer, meditation on Scripture, and intentional reflection are vital in aligning our daily lives with His teachings and promises. This spiritual discipline creates a heart attuned to God's voice, ready to respond to His guidance in every situation.

Visualizing what life looks like when fully aligned with Christ helps reinforce our commitment to abiding. By seeing the possibilities of a life steeped in His presence, we can aspire to live more faithfully, drawing strength, wisdom, and joy from our relationship with Him. This vision creates a compelling image of transformation, motivating us to pursue deeper intimacy with Christ and encouraging us amid distractions or challenges.

A life fully aligned with Christ is rich with spiritual fruits as noted in Galatians 5:22-23—love, joy, peace, patience, kindness, goodness, faithfulness, gentleness, and self-control. These qualities naturally emerge from an abiding relationship, influencing our relationships and interactions and creating a foundation of integrity and grace.

Abiding continuously also transforms our perspective, encouraging us to see each moment as an opportunity to reflect Christ's love and truth. Whether in everyday tasks or significant life events, our faith becomes intertwined with our identity, ensuring that everything we do honors God and exemplifies His character.

In moments of doubt or distraction, turning to Christ for renewal and support reinforces our abiding journey. Psalm 16:8 offers encouragement: "I keep my eyes always on the Lord. With him at my right hand, I will not be shaken." This assurance fuels our resolve, reminding us of the steadfast presence and strength available through our relationship with Him.

Today, take time to envision the impact of continuously abiding in Christ. Consider how strengthening this connection could transform your responses, decisions, and relationships. Invite God to renew your commitment and show you practical ways to nurture this abiding presence daily.

As you embrace this vision, may you experience the abundant life Christ promises, marked by peace, purpose, and profound joy. Carry this inspiration forward, living each moment as a testament to His sustaining grace, and inviting others to witness and experience the transformative power of abiding in Christ. Let this journey draw you closer to God's heart, unfolding into a life fully integrated with faith and overflowing with His love.

Abiding Practice: Picture Abundance

Today, take time to visualize what your life looks like when aligned in continuous abiding, embracing the abundance God offers.

1. **Find a Quiet and Inspiring Space**: Choose a place where you feel relaxed and inspired. It could be a cozy corner in your home, outside in a garden, or any setting that fosters creativity and reflection.

2. **Pray for Open Vision**: Begin by inviting God to open your heart and mind to envision a life fully aligned with Him. Ask the Holy Spirit to guide your thoughts and fill you with imagination inspired by His promises.

Example Prayer:
"Lord, as I visualize a life of continuous abiding, open my heart to the abundance You promise in Your presence. Help me see the beauty and purpose of a life fully aligned with You. Amen."

3. **Visualize a Life Abiding in Christ**: Envision yourself living each day rooted in Christ's love and guidance. Picture the effects of continual abiding in different areas of your life—relationships, work, service, and personal growth.

4. **See Relationships Flourish**: Visualize how your relationships might thrive through consistent love, patience, and forgiveness inspired by Christ. Imagine the harmony and joy that result from being fully present and connected to others through His love.

5. **Imagine Purposeful Living**: Picture yourself engaging in work and activities that align with God's purposes, utilizing your gifts to make a meaningful impact. See the sense of fulfillment and direction that comes from living in sync with His will.

6. **Envision Abundant Peace and Joy**: Visualize experiencing profound peace and joy, even amid challenges, as a result of abiding in God. Picture a life free from anxiety, grounded in His promises, and filled with gratitude.

7. **Commit to Continuous Abiding**: As you conclude your visualization, offer a prayer of commitment to nurturing a lifestyle of continuous abiding, seeking to actualize this vision in partnership with God.

Example Reflection and Prayer:
"Thank You, Lord, for the vision of an abundant life entwined with Your presence. Help me continuously abide in You, aligning my life with Your love and purpose. May Your influence transform every aspect, bringing glory to Your name. Amen."

By picturing abundance in a life aligned with continuous abiding, you reinforce your dedication to living in God's presence intentionally and joyfully. Let this practice inspire you to pursue a deeper connection with Christ, experiencing His abundant life in all you do.

WEEK 6: CONTINUAL ABIDING

Day 40: Abiding in Christ's Future

Principle: Abiding in Christ's Future

Abiding in Christ involves trusting Him not just with our present but with our future. It means living with confidence in His promises and guidance, believing that He holds our tomorrows in His hands. Jeremiah 29:11 assures us, "For I know the plans I have for you," declares the Lord, "plans to prosper you and not to harm you, plans to give you hope and a future." This trust in God's future plans invites us into a deeper reliance on His wisdom and love, freeing us from anxiety and opening us to His unfolding purposes.

Committing our future to God fosters a lifestyle of faith and expectancy, recognizing that each day is a step in His grand design. By daily reminding ourselves of His plans, we align our desires with His, nurturing a hopeful and proactive approach to life. This perspective encourages us to live with purpose, engaging with the opportunities and challenges before us with a confidence rooted in God's sovereignty.

Living with trust in God's future plans allows us to face uncertainty with peace and assurance. Philippians 4:6-7 encourages us to present our requests to God, accompanied by thanksgiving, allowing His peace to guard our hearts and minds. As we trust Him with the unknown, we find freedom from anxiety and rest in His faithful provision.

This trust calls for an openness to God's leading, challenging us to embrace change and seize new opportunities. It involves listening for His direction and being willing to step out in faith when He prompts us to act. Proverbs 3:5-6 reminds us to "trust in the Lord with all your heart and lean not on your own understanding," inviting us to submit our ways to Him and let Him make our paths straight.

Trusting our future to God also impacts our daily decisions, encouraging us to make choices that reflect His values and priorities. It's about seeking His kingdom first, as Jesus instructs in Matthew 6:33, trusting that as we focus on His purposes, everything else will be added to us in His perfect timing.

Today, reflect on how you can more fully trust God with your future.

Consider what fears or uncertainties you may need to surrender and invite Him to guide your decisions and plans. Pray for a heart that is responsive to His leading and open to the possibilities He places before you.

As you commit your future to God, may you experience a deeper sense of peace and anticipation, confident that He is orchestrating your life for your good and His glory. Let this trust inspire boldness and serenity, knowing that He is the author of your story, guiding you into a future filled with hope and promise. Embrace each day with expectancy, knowing that in His hands, your future is secure and purposeful.

Abiding Practice: Future Prayer

Today, embrace the principle of abiding in Christ's future by committing your future to God and reminding yourself daily of His plans.

1. **Create a Peaceful Setting**: Find a serene space where you can focus and connect with God without distractions. Allow this environment to foster openness and receptivity.

2. **Open Your Heart to God's Plans**: Begin with a prayer of surrender, expressing your desire to commit your future to God's hands. Acknowledge His control over your life and ask for trust in His plans.

Example Prayer:
"Lord, I commit my future to Your loving hands. Help me to trust in Your plans, believing that You have a purpose for every step I'll take. Guide me with wisdom and faith as I walk into the future You have prepared. Amen."

3. **Reflect on God's Promises**: Spend time reading and meditating on scriptures that speak of God's faithfulness and plans for your future. Allow His promises to shape your perspective and foster hope.

Example Verses:

- "And we know that in all things God works for the good of those who love him, who have been called according to his purpose." (Romans 8:28)

- "Trust in the Lord with all your heart and lean not on your own understanding." (Proverbs 3:5)
- "Do not be anxious about anything, but in every situation, by prayer and petition, with thanksgiving, present your requests to God." (Philippians 4:6)

4. **Visualize Your Future with Faith**: Imagine your life aligned with God's plans, entrusting your dreams and aspirations to His guidance. Picture yourself pursuing goals with confidence, fueled by faith in His provision.

5. **Commit Specific Areas to God**: Identify areas of your future where you seek God's direction—career, relationships, spiritual growth—and consciously place them in His care. Express your readiness to follow His leading.

6. **Daily Reminders**: Incorporate brief moments of future prayer into your daily routine, continually reaffirming your trust in God's plans. Use reminders—such as notes, scriptures, or alerts—to focus your mind on His promises.

7. **End with Gratitude and Assurance**: Conclude your future prayer with gratitude for God's faithful presence and the assurance that He is actively working in your life.

Example Reflection and Prayer:
"Thank You, Lord, for holding my future in Your hands. As I trust in Your plans, give me peace and courage to embrace the path ahead. Let my life be a testament to Your unfailing love and sovereign guidance. Amen."

By committing your future to God through prayer, you embody the principle of abiding in His eternal perspective and plans. Let this practice nurture a lifestyle of trust and hope, allowing God's wisdom to guide your journey with confidence and joy.

WEEK 6: CONTINUAL ABIDING: SMALL GROUP DISCUSSION GUIDE

Ice Breaker:

- Share a time when you had to forgive someone or ask for forgiveness. How did that process affect your relationship and personal peace?

Discussion Outline:

Day 36: Abiding through Forgiveness

- **Principle Discussion:** Discuss the importance of forgiveness in the Christian faith. How does forgiving others help deepen our abiding relationship with Christ?
- **Practice Reflection:** Share experiences from the forgiveness exercise. How did writing down past hurts and choosing to forgive impact your heart and perspective?
- **Application:** How can the practice of forgiveness become a regular part of your spiritual and relational life? Discuss practical steps.

Day 37: Abiding in Rest

- **Principle Discussion:** Explore the significance of rest as part of abiding in Christ. Why is it important to find time for rest in our spiritual journey?
- **Practice Reflection:** Reflect on the experience of resting in silence. What feelings or thoughts arose during those ten minutes, and how did the rest enhance your connection with God?
- **Application:** Share ways to cultivate regular rest amidst life's busyness. How can the group encourage each other to prioritize rest in various life rhythms?

Day 38: Abiding and Vision

- **Principle Discussion:** Discuss what it means to align with God's vision for our lives. How does engaging with God's vision reshape our sense of purpose?

- **Practice Reflection:** Share your thoughts or insights gained while dreaming with God. Did any new visions or purposes emerge during this reflective practice?
- **Application:** How can you stay aligned with God's vision for your life? Discuss ways to ensure your daily actions align with His purposes.

Day 39: Continuously Abiding

- **Principle Discussion:** Talk about what it looks like to continuously abide in Christ. How does this change the way we live our daily lives?
- **Practice Reflection:** Reflect on the visualization of an abundant life through continuous abiding. What aspects of your life resonated the most during this exercise?
- **Application:** How can you incorporate the idea of continuous abiding into everyday routines? Discuss specific habits to cultivate this lifestyle.

Day 40: Abiding in Christ's Future

- **Principle Discussion:** Explore the importance of trusting God with our future. What does it mean to live in anticipation of God's plans for us?
- **Practice Reflection:** Share thoughts from the future prayer exercise. How did committing your future to God bring comfort or clarity?
- **Application:** Identify areas of your life where you wish to trust God more with your future. How can daily prayer nurture this trust?

Closing Prayer: Conclude with a group prayer, asking God to help each participant apply the insights and practices discussed. Invite the group to share prayer requests that relate to living a life of continual abiding. Pray for strength, vision, peace, and trust as they walk deeper in their relationship with Christ.

CONCLUSION: THE BEGINNING OF A CONTINUOUS JOURNEY

Embarking on this 40-day journey of abiding in Christ has cultivated a deeper awareness of His presence, shaping habits that draw you closer to Him each day. Through dedicated principles and practices, you've taken intentional steps to weave His love, truth, and grace into the fabric of your daily life. These patterns of abiding have become a foundation—steady and supportive—in your spiritual walk.

Yet, as this structured journey completes, it's crucial to embrace this moment not as an end, but as the beginning of a continuous path of growth and transformation. The new habits you've established pave the way for an ongoing relationship with Christ that will only deepen as you continue to seek Him earnestly.

Just as a vine needs consistent care and attention to produce fruit, your spiritual journey requires ongoing nurturing and dedication. The practices introduced over these 40 days serve as guideposts—reminders of how to remain rooted in Christ amid both the blessings and challenges life presents.

Call to Continuous Abiding:

1. **Stay Rooted in Daily Practices**: Continue to implement the foundational practices that resonate most with you, such as prayer, scripture reading, or reflective meditation. Allow them to become ingrained routines of connection and renewal.

2. **Embrace Growth and Adaptation**: Recognize that seasons of life may call for adaptations in your spiritual routines. Be open to exploring new practices that align with your evolving relationship with God, allowing Him to lead you into deeper understanding and experience.

3. **Seek Community and Accountability**: Surround yourself with a community of fellow believers who will encourage your spiritual growth. Engage in conversations, studies, and fellowship that sharpen your focus and commitment to abiding in Christ.

4. **Remain Sensitive to the Spirit**: Cultivate a heart attentive to the Holy Spirit's promptings. Whether through gentle nudges or profound revelations, His guidance will steer you as you navigate life's complexities with faith and conviction.

5. **Pursue Continuous Learning**: Maintain a posture of learning and curiosity about God's Word and His ways. Dive into study, reflect on teachings, and apply insights that enrich your journey and broaden your understanding.

6. **Live Abundantly and Missionally**: Let abiding in Christ propel you into a life of purpose and mission. Reflect His love in every interaction, honoring His presence not only within you but also through you, impacting the world around you.

As you continue on this journey, remember that abiding is not about perfection but about pursuing Christ wholeheartedly. Every day is an opportunity to draw near to Him, to discover new depths of His love and grace, and to be transformed by His presence. Embrace this continuous path with an open heart and expectant spirit, knowing that as you abide, you align yourself with the abundant life God intends for you.

Let this be just the beginning of a lifelong journey of abiding—a journey marked by the joy, peace, and fulfillment found in the steadfast embrace of your Savior. May your heart always find its rest and purpose securely anchored in Him.